Ready-to-Use Resources for

GENIUSHOUR

in the Classroom

Ready-to-Use Resources for

GENIUSHOUR

in the Classroom

TAKING PASSION PROJECTS TO THE NEXT LEVEL

ANDI MCNAIR

Routledge
Taylor & Francis Group

NEW YORK AND LONDON

First published in 2019 by Prufrock Press Inc.

Published in 2021 by Routledge
605 Third Avenue, New York, NY 10017
2 Park Square, Milton Park, Abingdon, Oxon OX14 4RN

Routledge is an imprint of the Taylor & Francis Group, an informa business

Copyright © 2019 by Taylor & Francis Group

Cover and layout design by Allegra Denbo

ISBN: 9781032141862 (hbk)
ISBN: 9781618219015 (pbk)

DOI: 10.4324/9781003237600

Additional resources can be found a
https://www.routledge.com/9781618219015

Table of Contents

Section I

Introduction

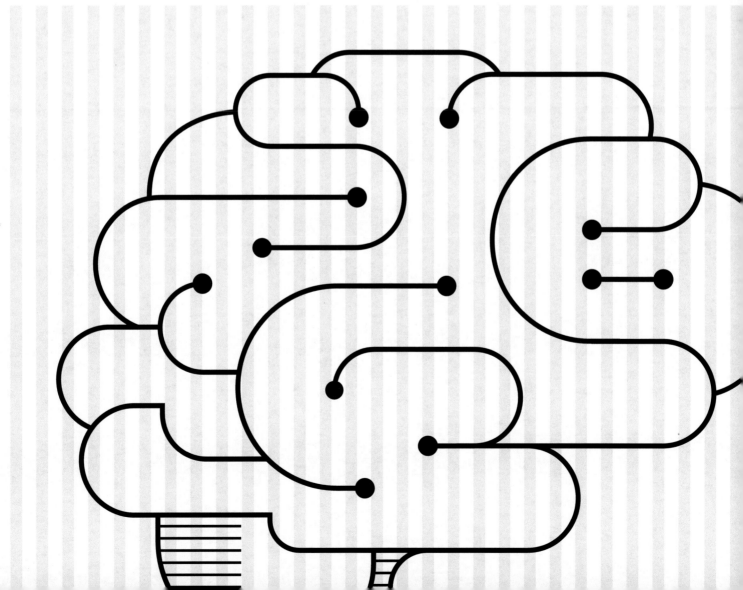

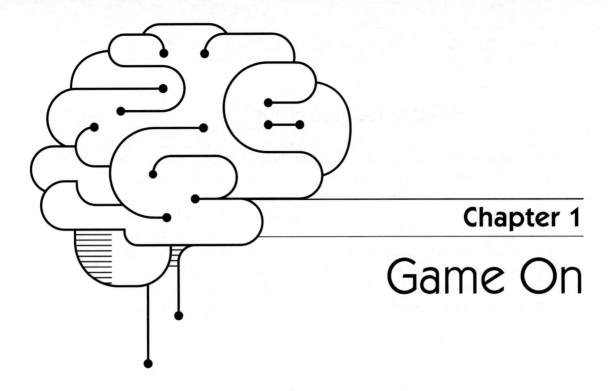

Chapter 1

Game On

Genius Hour . . . chances are that you've heard of passion-based learning and maybe even begun implementing some of the ideas behind Genius Hour, 20% time, or passion projects in your classroom. If not, passion-based learning is an opportunity for students to pursue their passions during the school day. It gives them an opportunity to connect learning to something that they would like to change, create, design, or impact. Because of amazing educators like Gallit Zvi, Denise Krebs, A. J. Juliani, Hugh McDonald, Joy Kirr, and Don Wettrick, I learned about Genius Hour and the impact it was having on the learners of educators who were making it a priority in the classroom. So, Genius Hour has been around for a while and has stirred up quite the conversation.

What if there was a way to level up? What if we could make Genius Hour even more meaningful and have an even greater impact on our learners? In writing the first book, *Genius Hour: Passion Projects That Ignite Innovation and Student Inquiry* (McNair, 2017), I simply wanted to introduce the 6 P's of Genius Hour—passion, plan, pitch, project, product, and presentation—and help educators understand why passion-based learning has the potential to create big change in today's classrooms. Now, it's time to go deeper, think bigger, and consider how we can use passion-based learning to create world changers.

DOI: 10.4324/9781003237600-1

What Is Genius Hour?

Genius Hour is really quite simple. Students choose a topic, a passion, or an interest. My students designed projects to learn more about animation, website design, animals, homelessness, sewing, and the list goes on. Whatever a student chooses to learn about becomes his or her project. Students then spend their time researching information, learning by doing, collaborating with experts, and designing a product that can be shared with an authentic audience. Although we called this time Genius Hour in my classroom, many classrooms prefer *passion projects* or *20% time*. Regardless of what it is labeled, it is a time for students to explore their passions through the creation of a product to share with the world.

Using the 6 P's

The 6 P's of Genius Hour—passion, plan, pitch, project, product, and presentation—is a process that has helped thousands of educators find their way as they begin to implement passion-based learning. It's a road map of sorts that makes the process manageable for educators and meaningful for today's learners. I had no idea when I began to use the process in my own classroom that it would have the impact that it has on classrooms all over the world. I just knew that I needed to do something in my classroom so that my students would be able to pursue their passions during the school day in order to experience real learning. (See Resource 1 for an educator's guide to the 6 P's.)

So, let's get right to it. What more could possibly be done? I mean, giving students an opportunity to pursue their passions is huge and a major mindset shift for educators. Frankly, it seems as close to the edge of the cliff as many of us would like to get. The cliff can be seen as many different things, but I think for me, it used to represent the control that I was holding on to. Before implementing Genius Hour in my classroom, I was only willing to go so far before I knew things might be riskier than what I was prepared to tackle. In the end, it took courage, willingness, and real drive to go beyond all that I had ever known as an educator. Ask yourself: What if you do go further? What if beyond that cliff is an opportunity to fly, soar, and experience learning like never before? What if on the other side of fear is a real opportunity to give your learners the tools, freedom, and ideas that they need to make an impact on the world around them?

RESOURCE 1

The Teacher's Role in Implementing the 6 P's

Passion	Use observation and conversation to help students find their passion, and encourage self-awareness by allowing them to pursue it.
Plan	Encourage students to plan and prioritize as they make decisions about when and how specific tasks will be done as they design their project.
Pitch	Give students the tools and time to share their ideas with the class, and build classroom culture by allowing them to offer feedback and advice to their peers.
Project	Allow students to collaborate with outside experts, work through failure, and use what is needed to work on their project during the time that is provided.
Product	Share student products on social media, school websites, or newsletters to encourage self-promotion and help them understand the value of their work.
Presentation	Encourage students to work on communication skills as they share their project successes and failures with the class and others outside of the classroom.

Preparing to Disrupt the Status Quo

I'm a big believer in disrupting the status quo. I'm always trying to think beyond what's comfortable, what's easy, and what we've always done. But it hasn't always been this way. I was a very complacent, traditional educator for a very long time. I did what I knew and didn't ask questions. However, today's learners made me question everything that I knew to be true about education and even question my own practice and core beliefs. I love to tell the story of when everything changed for me, and Genius Hour played a huge role in the mindset shift that needed to happen in order for me to give my learners what they needed for learning to be meaningful.

The first step to disrupting a system that doesn't work is to *stop doing what doesn't work anymore.* I think that what we've done so far in education is to continue to add to the plates of educators. In other words, we encourage educators to do *this*, do *that*, try *this new strategy*, and implement *this new technology tool*. However, we forget that if we are not taking anything off of teachers' plates, there's no possible way for them to add more, often times leaving no room for meaningful ideas and strategies.

It's almost as if we want to hold onto the things that we have done for so long just in case the pendulum swings the other way. I hate to give away the ending here, but I don't think that's going to happen. Instead, I think our learners are going to continue to push back on everything that we've done in traditional education, knowing that tradition simply will not prepare them for their futures. That being said, we must *stop separating content and innovation.* Instead, we must continue to find innovative ways to give our learners opportunities to explore the content as they learn by asking questions and applying what they know to figure out what they don't.

When I decided to implement Genius Hour in my classroom, I had to let go of many of the teaching strategies that I knew were not working. I knew that lectures and worksheets were not making the impact that I wanted on my learners. I also knew that learning by doing always had more of an impact. Although there are some traditional ideas and strategies that are beneficial and still work, I had to make some hard decisions. I had to take some things off of my plate. In order to implement Genius Hour, I had to see it as more than just fun time or free choice. I needed to find ways to weave in the standards and give my learners opportunities to practice life-ready skills, as well as create change and make an impact on the world around them. Sounds like a tall order, right?

How to Use This Book

Throughout this book, I plan to help you go deeper, go further, and face the fears that you may have about taking the leap into passion-based learning. I will share practical ideas to take passion-based learning to a level that will give learners an opportunity to not only pursue their passions, but also create change and make an impact in the real world. I will also share ready-to-use resources that you will be able to implement immediately in your classroom in order to make passion-based learning a reality for you and your learners.

I will describe how you can implement passion-based learning through an intentional and purposeful process. I hope that even if you are using the 6 P's of Genius Hour in your classroom right now, this book will give you new ideas and a fresh perspective that will give you the desire to take the next step, level up, and give your learners even more opportunities to make connections to content, the world beyond the classroom, and each other.

This first section concludes with some resources for beginning to implement Genius Hour. In Section II, each chapter involves a part of the 6 P's of Genius Hour process and includes the life-ready skills icons that most closely relate to that specific part of the Genius Hour process. See Resource 2 for an overview of the life-ready skills—collaboration, communication, creativity, critical thinking, and reflection. This resource can also be used as a classroom poster to introduce students to the skills. These skill icons are included at the beginning of each chapter to remind you of the importance of weaving the skills into the Genius Hour process and focusing on the skills as your students pursue their passions. This doesn't mean that you can't find a way to weave in other skills or that you are limited to only the skills that are identified. Later in the book, you will read more about the life-ready skills and how they can be used as students work on their projects. Until then, just be mindful of their importance and presence throughout the process. Chapters in Section II also include ready-to-use resources for each of the 6 P's. Section III covers important topics and resources related to managing Genius Hour and strategies for taking passion projects to the next level. Finally, Section IV concludes the book with some final thoughts.

Getting Started

Getting started with Genius Hour is not always easy, Parents, colleagues, administration, and even your students may not hop on board right away. You see, Genius Hour is different. It's not what you or your students have always

RESOURCE 2
Life-Ready Skills

COLL

Collaboration: Opportunity to work together to solve problems that may or may not have a right answer

COMM

Communication: Opportunity to practice eye contact, nonverbal cues, and listening skills

CR

Creativity: Opportunity to create, design, and/or produce

CR TH

Critical Thinking: Opportunity to think differently, apply learning, analyze a situation, and/or make judgments

REF

Reflection: Opportunity to connect with the learning by considering what was learned and why

Ready-to-Use Resources for Genius Hour in the Classroom © Taylor & Francis Group

done, and when you first explain that you are going to give your learners an opportunity to pursue their passions and learn by doing, it might sound like "free time" or just an opportunity for them to "play." With passion-based learning, one must truly experience it for him- or herself before understanding why it is important and how beneficial it can be in the classroom.

I was blessed to have supportive administration that allowed me to take a risk with Genius Hour, but I talk to many educators who do not experience that same support. Many times the pushback and doubt seem too much to overcome. However, if you can begin to weave aspects of Genius Hour into what you do in your classroom, I believe that it will be hard to deny the connections that are made and the learning that takes place. That being said, you must be willing to be intentional and purposeful about not only helping your students see and make those connections, but also being transparent in the process, so that parents, colleagues, and administrators can see Genius Hour for what it is. It isn't free time or play time; it is an opportunity for students to apply what they know by making connections and learning by doing.

The first thing that you need to do before introducing Genius Hour is obtain parent permission. Because Genius Hour is very different from what many of us experienced at school, you need to help parents understand *the why* behind passion-based learning and how their students will ultimately benefit from the opportunity. Resource 3 is a permission slip that can be shared with parents as you introduce Genius Hour and help them understand what will be involved in the process.

You may notice in Resource 3 that I didn't give parents an opportunity to say no. This is simply because rather than just providing a check box that gives them an out, you need to give yourself the opportunity to answer their questions and help them really understand what this will look like in your classroom with your learners. If after that conversation, they still are not on board, that is when you can consider them as not giving their permission for their child to participate.

You will also, if you have not already, need to introduce your students to the 6 P's. Resource 4 is a student handout introducing the 6 P's with space for students to write out responses. Resource 5 is a set of task cards for each of the 6 P's. These task cards can be used in place of the reproducible handout. They can be laminated or printed on card stock, saving you time and paper. Finally, Resource 6 is a classroom poster that can be used to display the 6 P's and serve as a reminder for your students throughout their projects.

Just as you should be when learning about any new, innovative idea, remain open-minded while reading this book. Although you might not be able to implement every single strategy, tool, or idea that is mentioned, I am certain that you will be able to take pieces of what is shared and consider how they can help you move your learners from creating projects to making an impact.

RESOURCE 3

Genius Hour Permission Slip

Dear Parents,

This year, your learners will be participating in Genius Hour. This will be an opportunity for them to pursue their passions during the school day while making connections to the standards. This time is built into our learning time so that your learners can explore new opportunities, learn new skills, and practice life skills that we know that they will need in the future. Please make time to ask about your child's Genius Hour project at home. Although students are only allowed to work on the project at school, they will have lots to share and talk about after they have spent time working on their project.

While working on Genius Hour, we will follow a process called the 6 P's. Students will find their passion, develop a plan, and pitch their idea to the class. Then, they will work on a project to develop a product and, finally, give a presentation. Much of our work will be done on a platform called Flipgrid. I will be sharing this grid with you all and would love for you to give feedback and comments to my learners as we move through the process.

Part of the Genius Hour process will involve your learner collaborating with an outside expert and sharing his or her work with the world. Both of these will be done in a way that is safe and will teach learners the importance of digital citizenship. If you have any questions about how this will be done and what tools will be used, please let me know.

Please sign below giving your permission for your child to participate in Genius Hour.

_____

_____ My child has permission to participate in Genius Hour, collaborate with outside experts, and share his or her work beyond the walls of the classroom.

_____ I would like further information about Genius Hour.

_____

Parent Signature

_____

Date

RESOURCE 4
Genius Hour 6 P's

1. **Passion:** What do you want to learn about? What do you think is interesting? What can you get excited about?

_____

_____

2. **Plan:** Who will be your outside expert? What materials will you need to complete the project? What will you need to do each day to reach your goals?

_____

_____

3. **Pitch:** How will you share your idea with the class? How will you get us on board?

_____

_____

4. **Project:** It's time to dive in! What do you need to do today to move forward with your project? What are you creating, making, or designing?

_____

_____

5. **Product:** What did you create? What can you show us to demonstrate your learning?

_____

_____

6. **Presentation:** How do you plan to share your learning? Can you share your idea or project with others? What tools will you use to make your presentation engaging for the audience?

_____

_____

1. **Passion:** What do you want to learn about? What do you think is interesting? What can you get excited about?

2. **Plan:** Who will be your outside expert? What materials will you need to complete the project? What will you need to do each day to reach your goals?

3. Pitch: How will you share your idea with the class? How will you get us on board?

4. Project: It's time to dive in! What do you need to do today to move forward with your project? What are you creating, making, or designing?

5. Product: What did you create? What can you show us to demonstrate your learning?

6. Presentation: How do you plan to share your learning? Can you share your idea or project with others? What tools will you use to make your presentation engaging for the audience?

RESOURCE 6

The 6 P's Poster

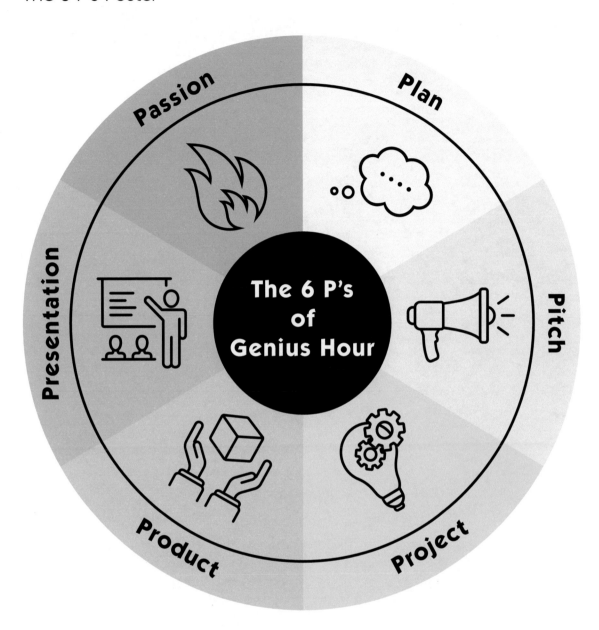

Section II

The 6 P's of Genius Hour

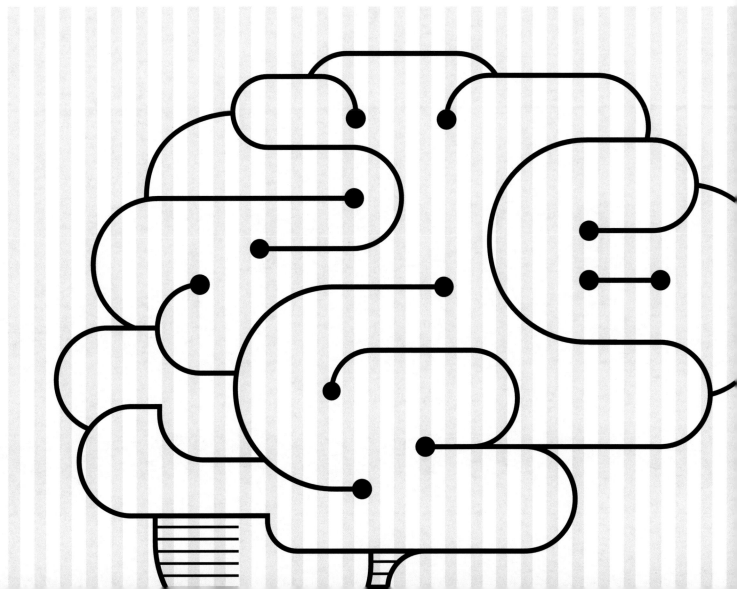

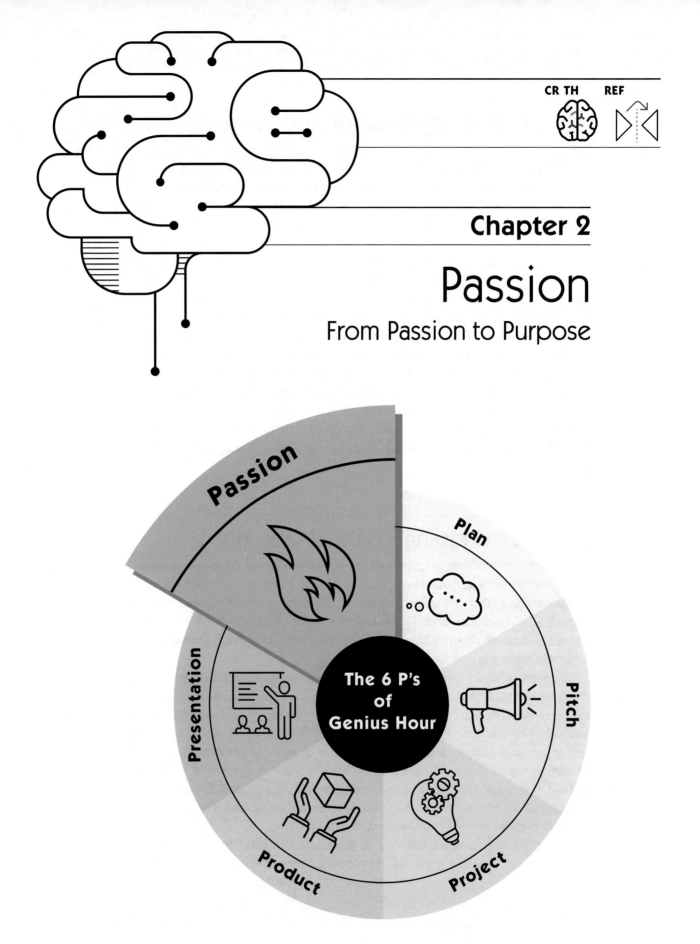

Chapter 2

Passion

From Passion to Purpose

DOI: 10.4324/9781003237600-2

Identifying Passions and Purpose

The first step in the 6 P's of Genius Hour is for learners to identify their passions. This is not always an easy task, as often students simply know what they are interested in, not what they are passionate about. They've never been asked what their passions are before, and it seems weird to consider the idea in the school setting.

Although starting with passion is very important, I want to encourage you to be willing to make *purpose* a priority as well. You see, without purpose, a student's passion will fizzle out very quickly. I recently read a wonderful analogy that compared both passion and purpose to a campfire (Derby, 2014). In the analogy, passion is represented by the flame that burns. It's bright, easy to see, and fun to watch. However, without the foundation, the wood that has to be present before lighting the match, there is nothing to support the fire.

It makes sense, doesn't it? In order for one's passion to ignite or stay ignited, there must be purpose. Purpose is the reason behind a Genius Hour project. Why is purpose important? Why does the student want to pursue this topic or idea? Purpose is what will continue to drive the project throughout the entire process.

Developing Essential Questions

If you've ever heard anyone talk about Genius Hour, you've probably heard someone share that a student's essential or driving question shouldn't be "Googleable." In other words, students shouldn't be able to research and find an answer to their question right away without really thinking through and considering whatever it is that they are trying to find.

Making essential questions a priority is one way to ensure that purpose is considered and identified before a learner jumps into a Genius Hour project. An essential question is a "question that is not answerable with finality in a single lesson or brief sentence" (McTighe & Wiggins, 2013, p. 3). Essential questions aim to provoke inquiry and spark even more questions. For example, "What should we eat as humans in order to be healthy?" is not an essential question. Instead, one might ask, "What does it mean to be truly healthy?" Essential questions are about so much more than simply learning the answer. They encourage learners to move toward learning how to learn.

Essential questions are not easy to write and can be difficult for students to understand. This is a great skill to practice before beginning Genius Hour.

Students can write essential questions for almost every learning experience. At the start of a lesson or unit, ask students to provide both examples and non-examples of essential questions as they pertain to the content that is being introduced. As students become better at recognizing and creating essential questions, they will begin to understand why such questions are important when developing the passion and purpose behind a Genius Hour project.

According to Watanabe-Crockett (2018), there are two things that can be done to make questions essential. First, move the question higher up on Bloom's (1956) taxonomy. In other words, an essential question should involve analysis and creation (higher levels of Bloom's taxonomy) rather than simple recall (the first level of Bloom's taxonomy). Taking a question to another level is often enough to make the question essential.

Also, remove specificity (Watanabe-Crockett, 2018). As previously explained, if there is a specific answer to the question, it's probably not an essential question. Essential questions should be open-ended and will oftentimes focus on the why. This can be difficult in a traditional classroom setting as we often focus on a specific answer. Essential questions are different and move beyond multiple-choice responses of A, B, C, or D, and into a bigger, broader scope that will give the learning real purpose.

Strategies for Identifying Passion and Purpose

Purpose gives learners something to work toward. Knowing why they are working on their project increases the likelihood that they will want to continue to move forward. Reminding students of the reason that they are working on their project is similar to stoking a fire. In doing so, you help the flame (passion) grow stronger and continue to exist. So how does a student find his or her purpose? Where do you start?

Thrively and Passion Bracket

Both Thrively and Juliani's (2013) passion bracket are the perfect places to start when it comes to finding a student's strengths and passions.

Thrively (https://www.thrively.com) gives students an opportunity to take a strengths assessment to identify and share their strengths and what they aspire to be. This information can be so beneficial, as oftentimes, students only see their strengths at school as skills and traits that are evident in the classroom. The same is true for the teachers. Sometimes, we miss out on the fact that our students can put a car back together or speak three languages simply because they aren't able to use those strengths in the classroom. However, if we know those strengths exist, we can use them to help our learners make connections. Using their strengths to address their weaknesses is always a good idea.

The passion bracket is another wonderful resource. This idea comes from Juliani (2013). Kirr (n.d.) has a great version of this resource on her Live Binder at https://www.livebinders.com/media/get/MTUzNDk5MTU=. The bracket is divided into two parts, Things That I Love and Things That Bother Me. Students narrow down interests in order to identify one thing that they love and one thing that bothers them. When those two things come together, a project idea can begin to stir. Although this process make take some creativity and conversation, the passion bracket can often lead to great ideas and real passion projects based on a purpose.

The Global Goals

One of my favorite resources to share with educators who are helping their learners find purpose is the Global Goals for Sustainable Development (Project Everyone, n.d.). These 17 goals—including no poverty, zero hunger, affordable and clean energy, and reduced inequalities—have been identified as opportunities to make the world a better place by the year 2030. The idea is that if we all contribute to ideas and solutions for the Global Goals, we can create real change and have a big impact on the world around us.

We know that this generation of students (Gen Z) wants to make a difference in the world (see McNair, 2019). They want to create change and have real opportunities to do so because of their connection to the world. Sharing the Global Goals with them helps them see beyond their classrooms, friendship circles, and homes. So many of our students aren't sure what change they want to create or what kind of impact they want to make simply because they are unaware of the problems that exist. They aren't always able to see beyond their own realities. Introducing the Global Goals takes students beyond their own realities and gives them a glimpse into the world around them. They are introduced to the idea of a better future and an opportunity to be a part of creating that better future.

Each of the goals is represented by an icon and resources to explore to learn more (see https://www.globalgoals.org). There are learning experiences designed for educators to make the goals a part of their classrooms and action steps to motivate and inspire those working toward solutions. The goals are found by clicking on "Schools" in the top menu and exploring the library of resources (see http://worldslargestlesson.globalgoals.org).

I often encourage teachers to introduce the Global Goals and ask learners to identify a goal that can be connected to their Genius Hour project. Because the resources are free, you can easily print out the icons grid, share it with your learners, and discuss which of the goals seems like something they can work toward solving. If you feel like it's too overwhelming, or have younger students, simply break the grid down and only introduce a few of the goals at once.

Take some time to explore the Global Goals and think about how you can use them in your classroom to encourage your learners to create change or make an impact. It's very possible that the goals will become the purpose behind their passion project and will be the foundation that is needed to keep the fire burning.

DIY.org and Wonderopolis

Students may also share personal experiences as the purpose behind their projects. They may want to create change based on something that they've experienced. For example, many of my students wanted to design projects that would address bullying on our campus. They had seen it or experienced it and wanted to make a difference by designing projects that would help solve the problem.

In *Genius Hour* (McNair, 2017), I also shared DIY.org and Wonderopolis as great places for students to explore concepts and project ideas. Students could combine these tools with the Global Goals to create a project that will make an impact. I love these tools as springboards for project ideas. Let me explain. Let's say a student finds a project on DIY.org that he or she wants to pursue. Ask the student if he or she can connect that project to one of the Global Goals. This requires critical thinking and the ability to make important connections between the content and the real world.

An example might be the Oceanographer patch on DIY.org (see https://diy.org/skills/oceanographer). Using the website, students are able to explore patches or skills. By completing the challenges, they are given the opportunity to earn patches for their achievements. DIY.org is no longer a free resource. However, you can access the different skills and activities for free. It's a wonderful place to get ideas or explore what exists beyond the walls of the classroom. One of the challenges included with the Oceanographer patch is Protecting the Oceans. This relates perfectly to Life Below Water in the Global Goals (Project Everyone, n.d.). Another example might be connecting the Mechanical Engineer patch on DIY.org (see https://diy.org/skills/mechanicalengineer) to designing solutions for Clean Drinking Water or Affordable and Clean Energy in the Global Goals.

The same process can be completed using Wonderopolis (see https://www.wonderopolis.org). Give learners an opportunity to explore and learn using the nonfiction articles that they find on Wonderopolis. Then, ask them to connect what they've learned to a Global Goal. For example, a student might explore "Why is World Hunger Still a Problem?" (see https://www.wonderopolis.org/wonder/why-is-world-hunger-still-a-problem) and connect what he or she has learned to the No Hunger and Zero Poverty Goals in the Global Goals (Project Everyone, n.d.).

Making these connections will help learners develop projects that give them an opportunity to not only pursue their passions but also fulfill their purpose. In doing so, they will be creating a sustainable project that they will want to work on because they are aware of the why behind what they are doing.

See the resources included in this chapter to make implementing some of these ideas even easier. Resource 7 will help students connect passion to purpose. Resource 8 is a Wonderopolis reflection resource, and Resource 9 will help students identify their passion and purpose.

RESOURCE 7

Connecting Passion and Purpose

1. What is something that bothers you?

_____

_____

_____

2. What is something that you could create or design to make an impact or change the thing that bothers you?

_____

_____

_____

3. What article did you read on Wonderopolis to learn more?

_____

_____

_____

4. Were you able to find a patch on DIY.org connected to your idea?

_____

_____

_____

5. What Global Goal could your project idea possibly impact?

_____

_____

_____

Name: _____ Date: _____

RESOURCE 8
What Did You Wonder? Wonderopolis Resource

Wonder Title: _____

1. How did you feel about this wonder?

2. What is a new vocabulary word that you learned from exploring this wonder?

_____

3. What does it mean?

_____

_____

_____

_____

4. Write 2–5 sentences to summarize what you learned from exploring this wonder.

_____

_____

_____

_____

_____

_____

_____

_____

Ready-to-Use Resources for Genius Hour in the Classroom © Taylor & Francis Group

RESOURCE 9

Passion and Purpose Identification

What is your passion?	How do you know?
What is your purpose?	How do you know?

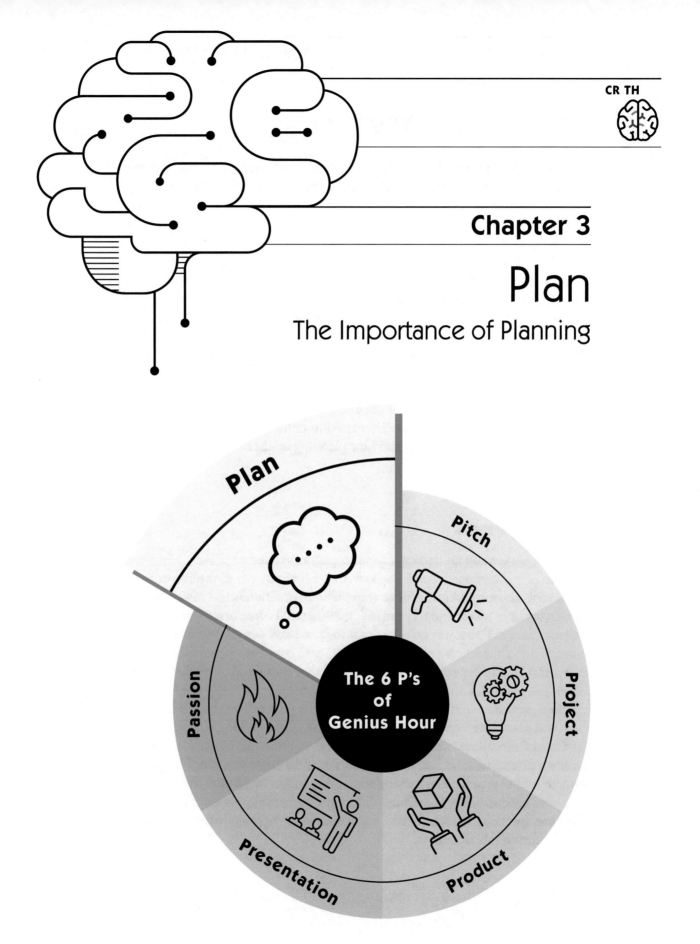

Chapter 3

Plan
The Importance of Planning

 DOI: 10.4324/9781003237600-3

Why Plan?

Planning is the easiest part of the Genius Hour process to skip. In the moment, it may seem like just an extra step to students as you ask them to really think through what their project will involve and what it might look like moving forward. However, if this step is skipped or overlooked, the project portion of Genius Hour will be much more difficult, and everything could fall apart.

When planning their Genius Hour projects, there are three aspects I asked my students to focus on. They had to share how long they thought their project was going to take, what materials they might need to be successful, and who they thought might be their outside expert for their project. Identifying their outside expert early on in the process gives time to begin to find the expert because they actually connect with the expert while working on the project portion of Genius Hour.

So, how do you take planning to the next level? I think you become even more intentional and purposeful about doing so. Planning is a real skill that students will need to use later in life. They need to understand its value as well as become aware of how they plan and how planning might be different for those around them.

Thought Partners

As a speaker and an author, I need to plan often and plan well. However, because of my personality and the way that I operate, my planning strategy might look chaotic and stressful to those who plan differently. I'm not one to lay things out in a neat and tidy outline, but instead, I often brain dump on my iPad and then use whatever comes of that to create and design. People often say to me, "I don't know how you think that way," or "I could never work like that." I always just laugh a little inside and think, well, then it's a good thing that I'm not asking you to do so. I don't expect others to plan the way that I do, and I actually benefit a great deal from working with those who plan differently. I learn from them and see things from a different perspective when working collaboratively.

One of my dearest friends, Kari Espin, is my thought partner. We work together often, and she helps me think and plan beyond what I originally thought and planned, often making something bigger and better than I could have ever imagined. She sees things differently and pushes me to think outside of my comfort zone and what's easy, and instead, plan to prepare for the difficult and uncomfortable situations.

I like the idea of students having thought partners as they plan their Genius Hour projects. An article that I read in *Forbes* explained that a thought partner does three things:

1. Challenges your thinking.

2. Causes you to modify or change your paradigms, assumptions or actions

3. Has information or a way of thinking that provokes you to innovate or otherwise leads to value creation in your business, career or life. (Stanny, 2012, para. 2)

If a student identifies his or her thought partner in the planning part of the Genius Hour process, the student can be given the opportunity to consult with that partner at any time throughout the process. In doing so, the student will be practicing communication and collaboration, while being pushed to see things from a different perspective and provoked to be innovative and/or creative throughout the process

Planning Strategies

Giving learners a variety of options as they plan their projects is important. However, it's okay to have a specific set of questions for them to answer. Resource 10: Genius Hour Planning Form is an invaluable tool for students' planning. I would share this tool with your students as you explain what planning is and why it's important. Give them an opportunity to ask questions and think through what each of the questions will mean for them. Explain that planning is about taking the time to be proactive and intentional about not only meeting their goals, but making small gains each time that they work on their project. This same tool could be recreated using Google Forms so that your learners can respond digitally rather than on paper. It's simply a matter of what you and your learners prefer and have access to.

Planning can also be done using Google Keep (https://keep.google.com). Using tools that can be used beyond the classroom is always a good idea. Many school districts are going Google, and giving students an opportunity to use this tool to document and prioritize should be considered. Google Keep can be color-coded, can include checklists, and can be shared, making it absolutely perfect for the Genius Hour planning process. You can also assign labels to notes, which makes so much sense when organizing notes between the 6 P's.

RESOURCE 10
Genius Hour Planning Form

KWH

K What Do I Know?	W What Do I Want to Know?	H How Will I Find Out?

What Materials Will I Need?

Materials I Will Bring	Materials I Will Need

Outside Experts

Who might be the expert on this topic, and how will we contact him or her?

Expert	Contact Information

Project Timeline

How long do you think your project will take?

_____

How much time will you spend on your project each week?

_____

Resource 10: Genius Hour Planning Form, *continued*

Potential Roadblocks

Potential Roadblock	Potential Solution

Pitch Day Plan

How will you pitch your idea to the class? Will you need technology, props, etc.?

_____

_____

_____

_____

Who will your thought partner be, and why?

_____

_____

_____

_____

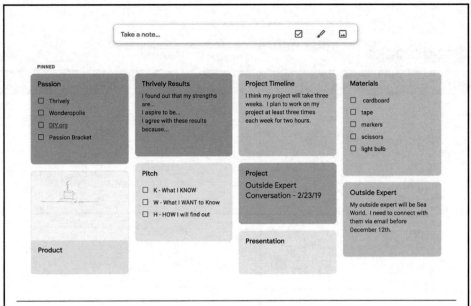

Figure 1. Example Google Keep notes. Google and the Google logo are registered trademarks of Google LLC, used with permission.

See Figure 1 for an example. I like the idea of students color-coding their notes in Google Keep to stay organized and represent each of the 6 P's. For example, students might code passion notes blue, plan notes green, pitch notes yellow, etc. Students could also use the labels that were mentioned earlier to organize their notes. Remember to give options and give students the opportunity to decide what will be best for them and how they think.

Setting Goals

Another important part of planning is setting goals. Goal-setting isn't always easy, but when it's not considered, students don't have a target. Giving your students a framework for setting their goals is a good idea in that it helps them remember what they are striving to achieve. With something as big and broad as passion-based learning, students can easily lose sight of what they originally set out to achieve, and goal-setting can help learners remain focused as they make strides to reach their goals.

SMART Goals

One of the most popular frameworks for goal-setting is SMART (Mind Tools Content Team, n.d.). SMART goals are specific, measurable, attainable, relevant, and timely.

Specific. A specific goal is similar to the center circle on a dartboard. You will not be able to be on target 100% of the time. Instead, you will land somewhere close to that target but still achieve some sort of change or impact by doing so. Although an essential question may be broad and unspecific, some specificity in the goals that are set is important so that learners will know if and when they actually reach their targets.

Measurable. Creating measurable goals is another way to ensure that learners will know when they've reached their goals. This is a way to identify what success or completion will look like for a specific project idea. Measurable goals are essential to measuring progress, and when the goal is specific and measurable, it is much more likely to be achieved (YourDictionary, n.d.).

Attainable. Learners need to know to create achievable goals. Although we want them to dream big and do big things, we also want them to understand that in order to create change or make an impact, they must be realistic. Encourage your learners to think beyond the status quo but consider feasibility as well. In other words, you don't want them to work hard on something that never had a chance of working out. That being said, this means that failure is an option. It's okay for students to have lofty goals as long as they are willing to do the heavy lifting and persevere when things are difficult. This part of a SMART goal is about finding balance. Don't discourage a project idea because of your own inability to see the possibilities. Instead, ask questions and guide your learners to think about how achievable the goals might be, and support them if they decide to continue to move forward.

Relevant. Relevance relates closely to purpose. It gives learners an opportunity to consider why a goal is important to them. Remember, without purpose, a passion will fizzle out very quickly, and that is why it is so important for learners to consider why their project idea is relevant. It is the why that will drive them to push through when tasks get difficult and continue to work even if they begin to lose focus.

Timely. Finally, a goal should be timely. Considering how long a project will take is a very important part of the planning portion of Genius Hour. Will the project take 2 weeks, 2 months, or 2 semesters? Although students may have difficulty setting a specific date, just having an idea of how long they might spend on their projects holds learners accountable. This also gives them an opportunity to practice time management as they do their best to stay on schedule and complete their project in a timely manner.

FAST Goals

Although I like the idea of SMART goals and think that they can be used to plan a project well, I recently learned about FAST goals. I wanted to share both with you, as what works in one classroom might not work in another. FAST goals involve frequent discussions, ambitious ideas, specific metrics, and transparency (Schneider, 2018). All of these factors are so important for learners to consider as they work on their projects and could be introduced to encourage goal-setting in the Genius Hour process.

Frequent discussions. Obviously, if you are passionate about something, you are going to want to talk about it. Think about your learners who you know are passionate about specific concepts and ideas. They often will use any opportunity that they can to weave their idea into the conversation. Keeping Genius Hour projects on the forefront helps learners make connections and continue to think about their project even when they aren't working on it. I think it's so important for students to learn through application. Frequently discussing Genius Hour projects encourages learners to connect content to their projects. You need to be intentional about giving students opportunities to use what they are learning outside of Genius Hour to learn by doing when they are working on Genius Hour.

Ambitious ideas. Ambitious goals push learners to challenge the status quo and set their expectations high. In doing so, you encourage your learners to be innovative, try new things, and take risks as they pursue their passions and word toward creating change or making an impact. Taking the easy road or path of least resistance is what many of our learners know of their school experience. They want to do whatever it takes to get an A or be successful as far as grades go. However, Genius Hour should encourage learners to do the opposite. They should be encouraged to step outside their comfort zones to take risks and try new strategies in an effort to meet their goals.

Specific metrics. Similar to SMART goals, FAST goals should be specific. Again, without the specificity, there will be no way to know when a goal is met. Being specific when setting a goal helps learners see that target and realize when they are getting close to the target.

Transparency. Finally, a FAST goal should involve transparency. Student goals should be shared and visible to their peers, outside experts, and anyone involved in helping them with their project. Being transparent encourages learners to be willing to ask for help when it is needed and share their struggles in an effort to collaborate and learn from others as they work toward a solution. Collaboration should play a huge role in any Genius Hour project, and being transparent opens the door for that to be the case.

Resource 11 is designed to help students develop SMART goals, and Resource 12 is designed for students to develop FAST goals.

Remember that planning is about helping students understand the importance of thinking ahead. Taking Genius Hour to the next level is all about using meaningful tools and giving students options regarding how they plan. Because setting goals is an important part of the process, be willing to allow your learners to set goals that work for them. Planning doesn't have to be perfect. It simply has to be an opportunity for students to organize and prioritize before they begin working on their projects. Don't assume that your learners think or organize the same way that you do. Share your thoughts and ideas but remain flexible as they explore ideas and tools to find what works best for them.

RESOURCE 11
Setting a SMART Goal

Project Title: _____

Essential Question:

_____

SMART Goal

Specific: What do you want to accomplish, and how will you make it happen?

_____

_____

_____

Measurable: What will be the result of you achieving your goal?

_____

_____

_____

Achievable: Is your goal realistic? How do you know?

_____

_____

_____

Relevant: Why is reaching your goal important to you?

_____

_____

_____

Timely: How long do you think it will take for you to reach your goal?

_____

_____

_____

RESOURCE 12
Setting a FAST Goal

Project Title: _____

Essential Question:

_____

FAST Goal

Frequently Discussed: How will you share your goal with others and talk it about it often?

_____

_____

_____

Ambitious: What risks are you taking with your goal?

_____

_____

_____

Specific: What do you want to accomplish, and how will you make it happen?

_____

_____

_____

Transparency: How will you share your goals with others and make collaboration a priority?

_____

_____

_____

Timely: How long do you think it will take for you to reach your goal?

_____

_____

_____

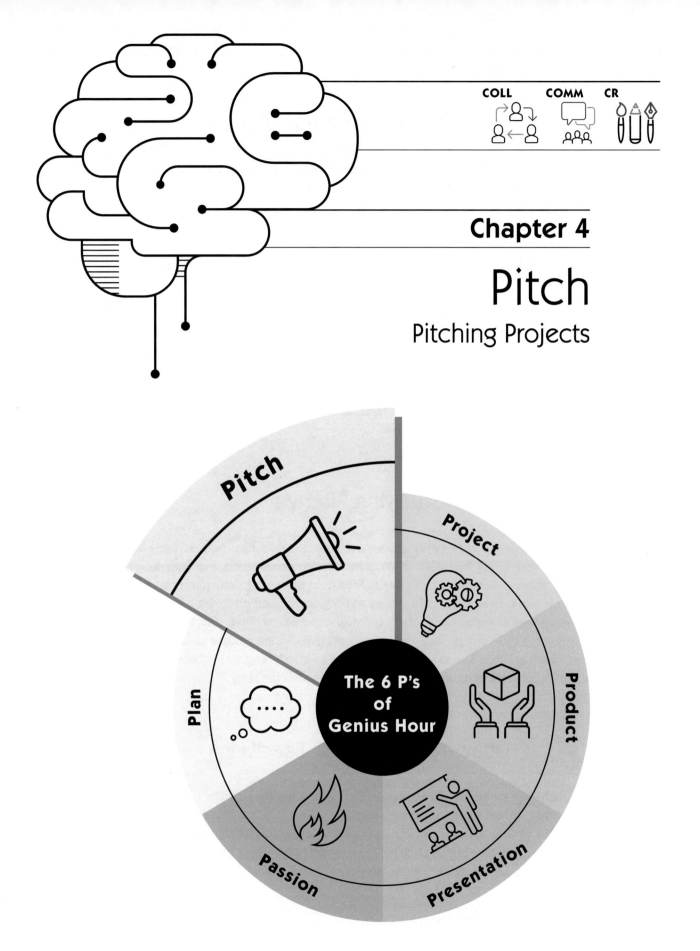

Chapter 4

Pitch

Pitching Projects

DOI: 10.4324/9781003237600-4

Preparing for Pitch Day

Pitching a project idea is an authentic experience that enables learners to practice communication and persuasion skills. Pitch Day is basically an opportunity for students to convince the teacher and their peers that their Genius Hour project is a good idea.

If you read *Genius Hour* (McNair, 2017), you'll remember that when students pitch their ideas, they should share their KWH—what they already know, what they want to know, and how they are going to find out more. In an effort to teach my students to be clear and concise, they had only 2–3 minutes to share these ideas. They could do so by using any tool or props that they felt were appropriate. Remember, students are building *their* project idea, and pitching is an opportunity for them to share their passion with their peers. They will be both nervous and excited. So, be patient and willing to listen. Offering feedback in the form of questions rather than giving advice is best, as this will remind students that this process is about them and what they are willing to do versus what you think will and will not work.

Studying Pitches

Most learners have never experienced pitching an idea before. They are familiar with being told what to do, when to do, where to do, and how to do. Giving them the freedom that they will have in preparing their pitch can be a little bit scary. In order to help students recognize a good pitch, it's a good idea to encourage them to watch the television show *Shark Tank*. Ask students to critique the different pitches and pay attention to which pitches are successful and which are not. You can use Resource 13 to give learners an opportunity to intentionally reflect on the experience as they watch the show.

Utilizing Flipgrid for Feedback

Although many educators make Pitch Day a big deal, this is not always a possibility. In talking to so many educators about Genius Hour and what it looks like in their classrooms, I've learned that many teachers do not have time to dedicate an entire day or class period to students pitching their Genius Hour project ideas. Giving up an entire class period of instruction just isn't something

RESOURCE 13
Shark Tank Reflection

Product: _____

1. What did you like about the pitch?

_____

_____

_____

_____

2. What did you dislike about the pitch?

_____

_____

_____

_____

3. Was the pitch successful? Why or why not?

_____

_____

_____

_____

4. What did you learn from watching this pitch?

_____

_____

_____

_____

that they can sacrifice. The other issue is that as students begin moving through the 6 P's of Genius Hour, the chances of them all being ready to pitch on the same day is slim to none. So, how can students pitch at different times while still giving everyone in the class an opportunity to both hear and offer feedback on their pitch?

Flipgrid to the rescue! If you haven't heard of Flipgrid, you can thank me later. This educational technology tool has made quite the name for itself in the past couple of years and can be so beneficial in the Genius Hour process.

Flipgrid is a place for students to share their thoughts and ideas. As an educator, you can create a grid with several topics. Within those topics, learners are able to communicate and collaborate via video. After a video is shared, others are able to offer feedback or respond to the video. If you're thinking that this would be perfect to use as your students pitch their ideas, you are exactly right. Setting up a pitch grid is a great idea. As students are ready to pitch, they simply visit the grid, record their pitch, and then wait to receive feedback from their teacher and their peers.

Giving feedback is a very important skill that today's learners need the opportunity to practice often. It might be a good idea to give them sentence stems within the Flipgrid topic to use when giving feedback to their peers. For example, instead of saying, "I don't like your idea," a student might respond with "I'm not sure if that will work. Have you thought about . . . ?" Rather than replying with a short, "Great idea," a student might say, "I really like where you are going with this because. . . ." Once students become familiar with what effective feedback looks like and how it can impact a project, you will no longer need to offer the stems. However, students may not be comfortable giving feedback to their peers simply because they are not given the opportunity to do it often.

If you decide to use Flipgrid to house student pitches, when students finish their work early or have already mastered what you are teaching, you can ask them to hop onto Flipgrid, watch the pitches, and leave feedback for their peers. What a great way to practice communication skills, giving and receiving feedback, and learning from others through collaboration!

Planning a Pitch

Although students will be anxious to share and sometimes ready to jump right in, just hopping on and recording on a whim is not a good idea. Students need to think through what they are going to share and what they want to communicate as they share their pitch. Please utilize Resources 14 and 15 to help students do just that. Resource 16 is a form for students to use as they offer feedback for their peers after watching and hearing their ideas.

Next-Level Pitching

Taking pitches to the next level means giving students access to a broader audience. After pitching several times, students will become comfortable with the process, and it will be easy to just hop on Flipgrid or stand in front of their peers and go through the motions. When this begins to happen, it's time to take things to the next level. Consider sharing your students' pitches with experts in their field or community members. Give learners a different audience and an opportunity to receive feedback from those beyond the walls of the classroom. Remember to obtain parent and administrative permission before doing so, but sharing pitches beyond the walls of the classroom can prove to be very valuable. Students will obtain a different perspective and real feedback from those that know the most about what they are sharing.

RESOURCE 14
Pitch Checklist

Directions: Please include the following information when presenting your pitch to your peers. You will have 3–5 minutes to share the following information.

- ❏ Project Title
- ❏ **KWH**
    - ❏ **K**—What do you already know about this project, concept, or idea?
    - ❏ **W**—What do you want to know about the project, concept, or idea?
    - ❏ **H**—How are you going to find out what you would like to know about this topic?

- ❏ Why did you choose this project?
- ❏ How can your peers support you as you work on your project?
- ❏ What do you hope to create as a product to represent your project?
- ❏ Other things to consider:
    - ❏ **Props**—What props will you use, if any, during your pitch?
    - ❏ **Technology**—What technology will you need to deliver your pitch?

Name: _____ Date: _____

RESOURCE 15

Pitch Form

Project Title: _____

    1. **K**—What do you already know?

    _____

    _____

    _____

    2. **W**—What do you want to know?

    _____

    _____

    _____

    3. **H**—How are you going to find out?

    _____

    _____

    _____

    4. Will you need any props for your pitch?

      ❑ Yes _____

      ❑ No

    5. What will you use to create your pitch presentation? (Check one.)

      ❑ Powtoon   ❑ Vidra   ❑ Google Slides   ❑ iMovie

      ❑ Other _____

Other technology that you will need for your pitch:

_____

_____

_____

RESOURCE 16

Pitch Feedback Form

Project Idea: _____

1. How do you feel about this project idea?

   _____

   _____

   _____

   _____

2. Explain why you feel that way.

   _____

   _____

   _____

   _____

3. What do you love about the project idea?

   _____

   _____

   _____

   _____

4. What advice would you give about the project?

   _____

   _____

   _____

   _____

Chapter 5

Project
Purposeful Projects

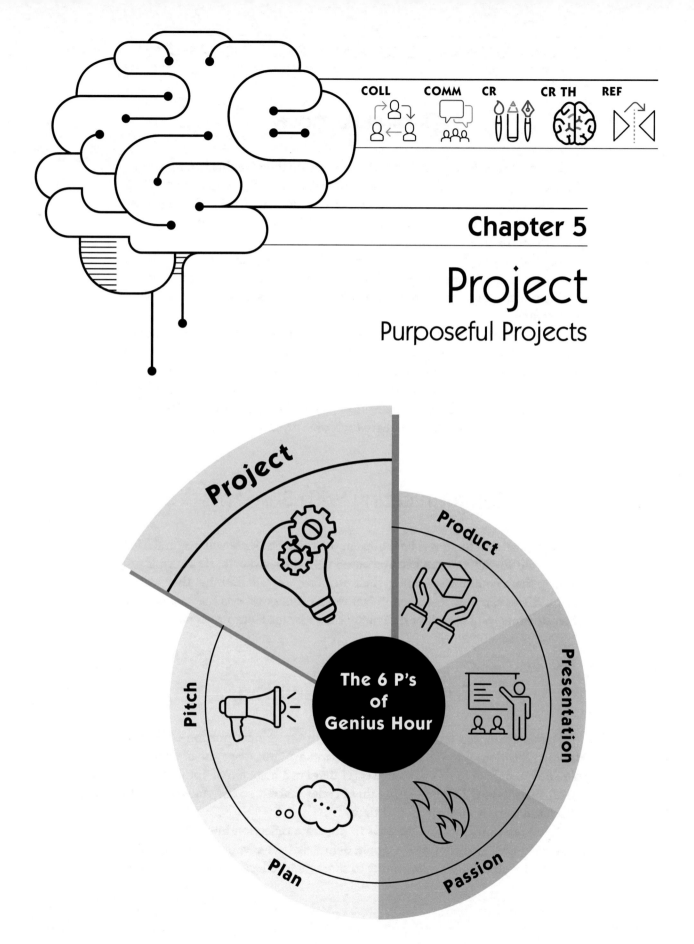

DOI: 10.4324/9781003237600-5

Finding Purpose

When it's time for students to begin working on their Genius Hour projects, you will be able to sense the excitement. Your learners will be ready to get their hands dirty, dive into their projects, and begin doing the work. Although they may be a little nervous and afraid of "messing up," you need to support them by giving them the freedom that they need to learn by doing.

As students begin working on their projects, give them opportunities to remember their purpose every chance that they get. Remember, that purpose is going to drive them to continue working and ask questions that will result in real learning.

Taking project time to the next level involves asking higher level questions and helping learners make connections to their purpose. In doing so, you are giving them a reason to want to learn and reach a deep level of understanding. Genius Hour is really an opportunity for students to move beyond surface level and dive deep into learning by application. When they begin to dive deep, they will begin to take ownership and drive their own projects.

Communicating With Students

Recognize that there will be bumps in the road. Students will become frustrated, want to quit, or even become bored with their projects. However, if you can help them continue to hone in their purpose, you will find that they will be more likely to carry on. Resource 17 features a list of questions that you can ask when students want to quit or give up on their Genius Hour projects.

Encouraging Reflection

Hands down, the most important piece to the project portion of Genius Hour is reflection. Without reflection, students will not make the connections that you need them to make. It's no secret that I'm a huge fan of Tony Vincent's (2013) Reflection QR Codes. Using these codes make it so easy for learners to reflect and learn from their project time.

There are so many different ways to integrate reflection into Genius Hour. If I were in the classroom now, I would definitely take advantage of Flipgrid in order to give students an opportunity to share their reflections with each other.

RESOURCE 17

Student Conference Questions

1. How do you feel about your project right now?

2. Why do you feel that way?

3. Why did you begin working on this project?

4. Have you accomplished your goal with this project?

5. What do you need to do right now to move forward?

6. What can you do next time things become difficult?

7. Why were you excited about your project when you first developed the idea?

8. What will happen to your purpose if you give up now?

9. What change might you create if you persevere?

10. How will you feel if you give up on your idea now?

Creating a reflection grid is so easy and just makes sense. At the end of each project time, you could allow students to take 3–5 minutes to get on Flipgrid and share what they learned and how they will use that learning moving forward. When reflecting on Flipgrid, students will learn from each other how to reflect well and will make connections to each other through the experience.

Remember to be flexible and offer variety when encouraging students to reflect. Communication, writing, and collaboration are all important when reflecting. In an effort to help you give them these opportunities, I've created a reflection cube for you to use with several different options (see Resource 18: Reflection Cube). Ask students to roll the cube and reflect in the way that is suggested on the side that they land upon:

- **Reflect with a friend:** Reflecting with friend gives learners an opportunity to practice communication and collaboration. Give them a couple of minutes to turn and talk at the end of class to share their reflections. You can give them prompts or allow for open reflection.

- **Reflect on Flipgrid:** As described above, students can reflect by recording videos and sharing them on the grid. In doing so, they will be able to practice communication skills and the ability to be clear and concise.

- **Reflect by blogging:** Using tools such as Kidblog and Edublogs, students can reflect through writing. Because blogs are digital, they can be shared with an authentic audience, giving learners access to the world beyond the classroom.

- **Reflect on a sticky note:** Sticky note reflections force learners to find focus and narrow their thoughts down to a single reflection. Create a space for students to post their sticky notes and read those posted by their peers.

- **Reflect on Padlet:** This is simply a digital way for students to post a sticky note. Creating a reflection Padlet (https://padlet.com) gives students the option to share with an audience as a Padlet can be shared with a link or QR code.

- **Reflect through a sketchnote:** Reflection doesn't have to be fancy. It can be as simple as sketching out what was learned. In a journal or on a mobile device, students can sketchnote their reflections for the day. Assuming that this generation prefers technology all of the time is a mistake. Journaling and sketchnoting may be a breath of fresh air for many of your learners.

RESOURCE 18

Reflection Cube

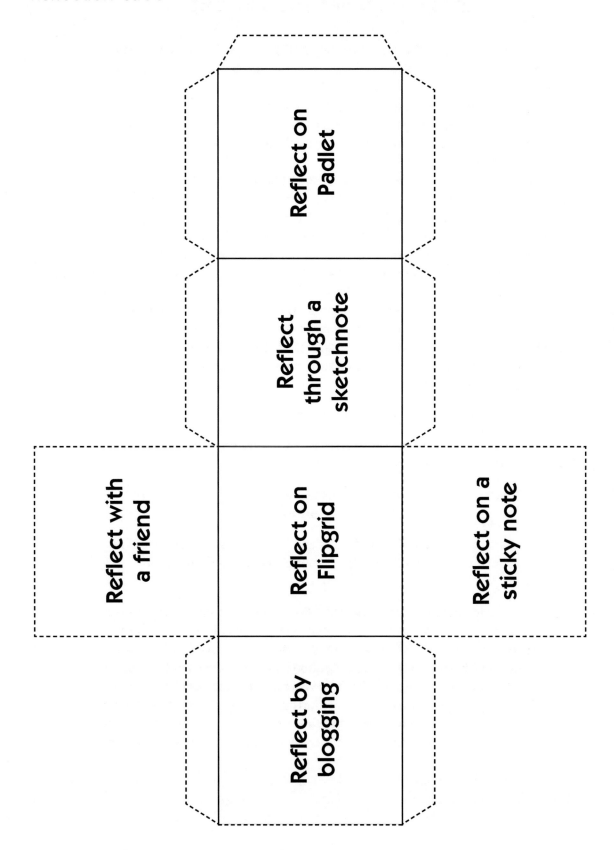

Considering Benefit Mindset

Just after writing *Genius Hour* (McNair, 2017), I learned about a new mindset known as *Benefit Mindset.* As I read about it and began to connect with other educators like Robert Ward (@reWARDingEDU) who were making this mindset a priority in their own classrooms, I couldn't help but see the connection to Genius Hour. I was just beginning to think about this book and sharing the importance of purposeful projects. It was almost as if Benefit Mindset was the missing piece to the puzzle.

So, what is Benefit Mindset, and what does it have to do with Genius Hour? Benefit Mindset is described as a shift from wanting to be the best *in* the world to wanting the be the best *for* the world (Buchanan, 2016). Can you imagine the impact that this could have on today's learners if we could find practical ways to weave this mindset into the classroom? It simply makes sense to give students opportunities to want to do good and make an impact. That's what taking Genius Hour to the next level is all about.

Benefit Mindset resources are popping up everywhere and might be just what you need to make this a reality in your classroom. Spend some time diving into the idea of benefit mindset and consider how you might be able to integrate it not only in Genius Hour, but also into your classroom every day. Some worthwhile resources include:

- Benefit Mindset: http://www.benefitmindset.com

- "Exploring the Benefit Mindset" at Edutopia: https://www.edutopia.org/article/exploring-benefit-mindset

- "Better Off With a Benefit Mindset" at Getting Smart: https://www.gettingsmart.com/2017/05/better-off-with-a-benefit-mindset

- "Benefit Mindset: Why It Matters and How to Foster It in Your Classroom" at James Stanfield: https://stanfield.com/benefit-mindset

I love the idea of introducing Benefit Mindset by allowing students to collaborate and share ways that they have seen evidence of it at school. Ask them to share examples of experiences in which Benefit Mindset has made a situation better and when it would have made a situation better had it been put into place.

A couple of great videos on YouTube represent Benefit Mindset well and can also be a great place to start as far as introducing Benefit Mindset to your students. Ask them to count how many times they see someone use Benefit Mindset to impact others throughout the videos. Then, encourage real conversation about what the students have watched and the impact it had on them. See examples, such as https://www.youtube.com/watch?v=cZGghm wUcbQ and https://www.youtube.com/watch?v=nwAYpLVyeFU.

Let's take a closer look at Benefit Mindset and the role it might play in Genius Hour. Mindsets are important in the classroom and can have a huge impact on how a student reacts when faced with struggle or frustration. Although Carol Dweck's (2006) growth mindset is still very important and should be encouraged, Benefit Mindset takes growth mindset to another level by moving students from learners to leaders, focusing on the why rather than the how, and encouraging learners to meaningfully contribute to the world around them.

How do you see your learners? Have you ever thought about your perspective and considered seeing every single one of your students as leaders? In order to do this, we have to give them opportunities to lead. We must know them well and be willing to get out of their way. Understanding who they are beyond the walls of the classroom is the best way to recognize opportunities for leadership. Genius Hour gives you this perspective.

Not all students lead the same way. I have two boys who lead very differently. Our oldest son is quiet and leads by example. He tends to make good decisions and doesn't like to stand out. I was recently filling out a survey for National Honor Society and was asked about his leadership skills. At first, I panicked and thought, "Oh no, he's not a leader." But after reflecting and thinking on what I knew to be true about who he is, I realized that just the opposite is true. You see, he is a leader. He just doesn't lead by asking for attention.

By definition, *to lead* means to show someone the way by going in front or beside them. Although our eldest isn't the one out front asking everyone to follow, he is the one walking beside others as they try to find their way. He's quiet about his choices and doesn't prefer a great deal of attention. But if you look close enough, it's easy to see that he is a leader. One of my favorite quotes is "Never assume that loud is strong and quiet is weak." Don't make the mistake of assuming that your quiet learners can't lead. Instead, look for ways to give them leadership opportunities that make sense considering who they are.

Our middle child is a leader in every definition of the word. He does walk in front and tends to be a leader regardless of the situation that he is in. He is seen as a leader by his peers, and we are constantly reminding him that with that ability to lead comes a great responsibility to do it well. It's interesting because he doesn't always recognize his leadership. In other words, when we talk about leadership, he sees others as leaders and often struggles with realizing the impact that he has on those around him. Assuming that natural leaders are always comfortable in a leadership role is another mistake that we often make with our learners.

Take time to recognize your natural leaders and your quiet leaders. Find ways to turn all of your learners into leaders and encourage them to see themselves in that same light. Genius Hour will give them some perspective on what they can lead on and the impact that they can have on those around them. Don't miss the opportunity to help your learners make this connection as they pursue their passions.

Focusing on the why is easier said than done. We get so wrapped up in content and curriculum sometimes that we forget the importance of the why. Being purposeful about why we are doing something is always important but definitely imperative when it comes to Genius Hour. Remember, this why is the purpose and is the foundation to the projects that are designed and created by your learners.

Think about being an educator. We can easily lose sight sometimes and become frustrated or lost. We forget our why and lose focus. The fire begins to fizzle, and we begin to wonder why we do what we do. I don't know about you, but when this happened for me, I had to take time to reflect and refocus on my why. I asked myself why I did what I did. Why did I come to work every day? Why did I become an educator in the first place? To put it simply, my response was always my students. They were my why, and when I needed to stoke the fire, I went back to the foundation of the fire. I would simply remember my students and how big of an impact I had on their lives.

What does it mean to meaningfully contribute, and how many opportunities would you say that your learners have throughout the school day to do so? Before my mindset shifted, I was a very traditional educator. I have to admit that it was not often that my learners meaningfully contributed to anything other than a worksheet and a fun activity every once in a while, thrown in for good measure. It's difficult to admit, but this was the reality in my classroom. I missed opportunities for my students to take what they were learning beyond the walls of the classroom to make a difference in the world.

Benefit Mindset is focused on being intentional about giving students opportunities to meaningfully contribute to the world around them. It only makes sense to weave this into Genius Hour as students work toward making an impact or creating change around something that bothers them. Contributing to change by doing or taking action is something that today's learners need to experience. Remember, we know that this generation of students wants to make an impact on the world (McNair, 2019). Giving our students opportunities to meaningfully contribute puts them into the position to do that and so much more.

Building Life-Ready Skills

Weaving life-ready skills into Genius Hour is so important, as doing so helps our learners connect their learning beyond the walls of the classroom. The 6 P's of Genius Hour were designed specifically to create opportunities for my students to practice these skills throughout the process. I wanted to be intentional about collaboration, communication, creativity, critical thinking, and reflection every single day. These skills are the 4 C's (National Education Association, 2010) + 1 R. Sure, I had content and curriculum that I needed to prioritize, but weaving these skills into every learning experience that I designed, including Genius Hour, gave me an opportunity to make learning real.

As students work on their projects, there are so many opportunities to focus on these skills. Planning requires critical thinking and lots of reflection as students consider what will work best for them. Pitching gives them an opportunity to practice communication and collaboration skills. Think about the opportunity to connect with outside experts. What a great way practice real collaboration and communication while connecting with someone beyond the walls of the classroom. While working on a Genius Hour project, students should be given the opportunities to practice all of the life-ready skills. Being creative as they think critically to solve problems while collaborating and communicating with others is what passion-based learning is all about.

Taking Genius Hour to the next level is about creating change and making an impact. In doing so, students must learn to be empathetic and think of others. So often, their generation is described as selfish and self-absorbed. However, when given the opportunity they will often prove that just the opposite is true. In an effort to be intentional about giving them these opportunities, it's a good idea to add one more life-ready skill into the mix—kindness. How can kindness play a role in a project idea? Students can consider how they are doing something for someone other than themselves. In taking a project to the next level, students must move beyond what they want to do and, instead, focus on what's best for the outcome that they hope to create.

In Resource 19: Genius Hour Reflection Form, students are asked to identify the mindset as well as the life-ready skills that they used to move forward on their project. Using this resource each and every day that students work on Genius Hour gives learners the chance to really think about the work that they are doing and how they are using what they know to learn about what they don't.

Name: _____ Date: _____

RESOURCE 19
Genius Hour Reflection Form

Which mindset(s) did you use today?

Fixed   **Growth**   **Benefit**

Why did you choose the mindset that you chose?

_____

_____

_____

_____

Which life-ready skills did you use today?

COLL   **COMM**   **CR**   **CR TH**   **REF**   **KIND**

Explain.

_____

_____

_____

_____

What did you learn today?

_____

_____

_____

_____

Chapter 6

Product
Process Over Product

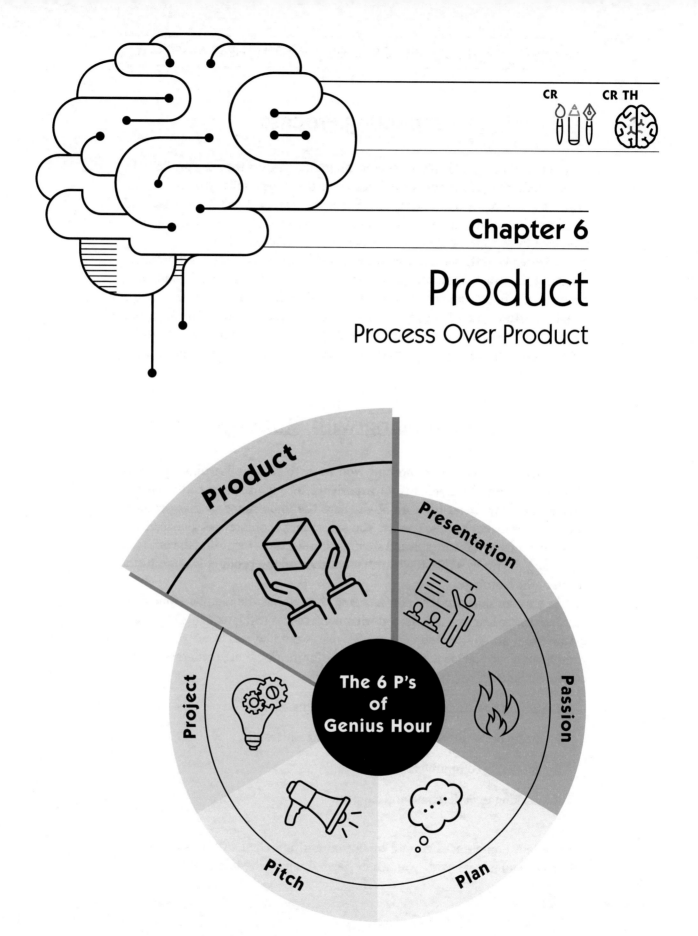

DOI: 10.4324/9781003237600-6

Respecting Process

Genius Hour should always be more about the process than the product. In other words, even if a product isn't created or the project falls apart before the product is complete, that doesn't mean that the learner didn't experience real learning. Understanding that Genius Hour is process over product helps educators react in an appropriate manner when such a situation arises.

We often hear the words *process over product* when discussing art projects. It's about the practice, emotions, and risk-taking that are involved while producing the product rather than the actual product itself. The same is true for athletics. Although the big game is important, the preparation for the big event requires the most focus, the most time, and the most willingness. It's in the practice that you learn, you grow, and you are able to fail in order to get better.

Conferencing With Students

Because process is so important, you need to provide learning opportunities throughout the Genius Hour experience through student conferencing. I have heard my friend Joy Kirr often share the importance of these conferences, and it makes so much sense. You see, student conferences give learners an opportunity to talk through and share their reflections regarding the process. It's during the process that the learning occurs, and the product is often just a result of the learning.

As you consider student conferencing throughout the Genius Hour process, help your learners understand what conferences will look like. Help them realize what an effective student conference looks like and what you expect from them when you meet. Some quick ideas for making these conferences successful include:

1. asking questions rather than always giving advice,

2. being open-minded and willing to think differently,

3. modeling communication skills, and

4. seeking to understand and support.

Student conferences should be casual and informal. Allow students to schedule conferences with you when needed, and schedule regular conferences with them to check in and see how their projects are progressing. These mini-conferences are similar to checking the oil in a car. Rather than waiting until the engine explodes, checking the oil often and changing it when it's time are important. The same is true for this type of learning. Checking in often gives you the opportunity to help make changes and support learners before things go completely wrong.

Conference with students as they work on each of the 6 P's. This means that throughout a project, you may conference with each student a minimum of six times. Remember, these aren't long conferences. These should be short check-ins for you to connect and find out where your students are and what they need from you. Below are some sample questions that you might ask along the way:

- **Passion:** How difficult has it been to identify your passion? What did you decide upon, and how do you know?

- **Plan:** What is your essential question, and what do you need from me to get started on your project? Share your SMART/FAST goal with me, and let's talk about how you can reach that goal.

- **Pitch:** How will you share your idea with the class? Will you be using any props or technology?

- **Project:** How is your project going? What's working, and what isn't? How can I support you as you continue to move forward with your idea?

- **Product:** What will you be creating to share with an audience? Who is your audience, and what impact do you hope that your product will have?

- **Presentation:** How will you share what you've learned with us? Will you be using any props or technology?

Document student conferences so that you are able to see growth and the results of what was discussed (see Resource 20: Student Conference Documentation). This also makes it easy for you to revisit trouble areas in follow-up conferences and conversations.

Name: _____ Date: _____

RESOURCE 20
Student Conference Documentation

Project Title: _____ Conference Date: _____

1. What's going well?

_____

_____

_____

_____

2. What's not going well?

_____

_____

_____

_____

3. How can I support you?

_____

_____

_____

_____

Other Notes:

_____

_____

_____

_____

_____

Remembering Audience

Products cannot always be seen, touched, or displayed. In taking Genius Hour to the next level, many of the products might be experiences. Two of my students developed the idea to host a 5K for our community to run as we raised money for local animal shelters. The 5K that they managed and put together was their product. It was documented through video and photos. This is just one example, but you can imagine the variety of products that will be created. Be open to new ideas and give students opportunities to produce what they feel will most represent what they learned throughout the Genius Hour process. Although many times products are posters, slideshows, or models of something specific, when you begin to ask students to create change or make an impact, that might change.

Help your learners to realize how to create appropriate products for their audience. Just like so many of the things that we've discussed in this book, this all comes back to purpose. Knowing why they are creating a product will drive what product they create. This is a great conversation to have in one of the student conferences that you schedule.

If students want to create change around a culture of bullying on a campus or within a district, they might introduce a campaign that is implemented throughout the school year. Students wanting to impact homelessness in their community might make connections or collaborate with city council. Their product might be a well-designed plan that is shared with the community to help create that change.

Again, be open-minded when it comes to products, and realize that the goal with this specific part of the Genius Hour process is simply about learners finding a way to demonstrate what was learned as they worked on their passion project. Give your students examples of products but encourage them to think beyond what you provide and be creative as they consider how they can best demonstrate what they learned and accomplished as they worked on their project.

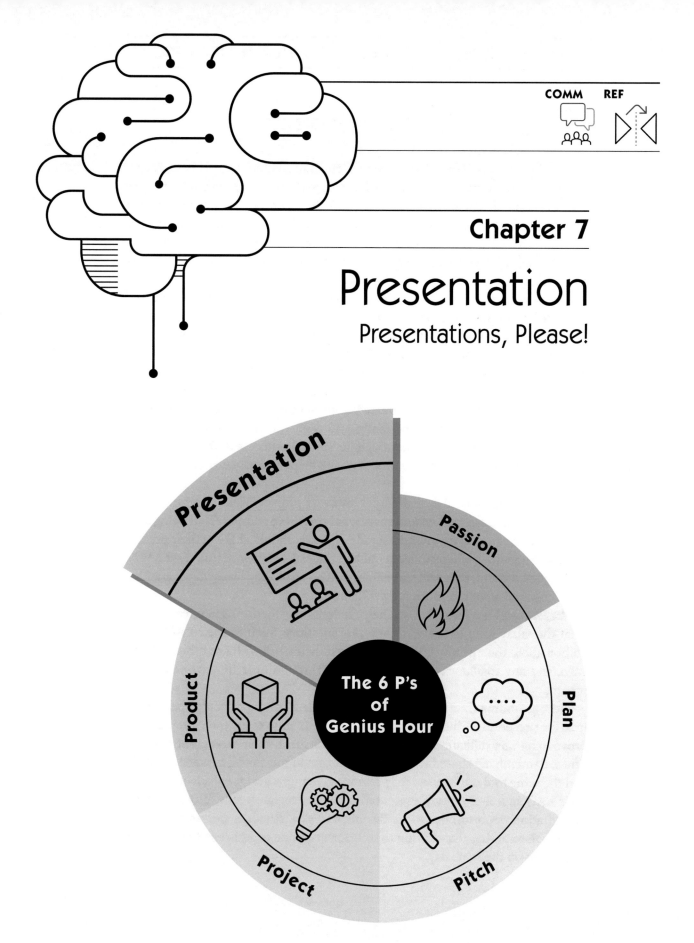

Chapter 7

Presentation

Presentations, Please!

DOI: 10.4324/9781003237600-7

Presenting Projects

The final piece of the 6 P's of Genius Hour is presentation. This is an opportunity for students to share what they have learned, as well as what actions they took to create change or make an impact. Although presenting can cause fear and anxiety for many learners, when done well and by letting the students have choice and voice, presentations can be an opportunity to develop communication and reflection skills that students will use well beyond the classroom in the years to come.

At its core, presenting is a time for students to reflect on what they learned throughout the Genius Hour process. Students can look in the rearview mirror and recognize what went well, what didn't go well, and, most importantly, what they learned throughout the process. Whether or not a project was successful should not determine whether or not students present. Even if a project tanks and doesn't work out in the way that was expected, that doesn't mean students just stop. They should still be expected to present on what went wrong, what they feel they could've done differently, and what was learned in the process. You see, that's the great thing about Genius Hour. In success or failure, learning still happens. You must be intentional about helping your learners recognize this.

Presentations should look different for every project. Make sure you do not dictate how students present and share what they have learned. That being said, it's a good idea to help them understand what they should share in their presentations. Remember, when students pitched their ideas, they shared their KWH. When they present, they will share their LAQ—what they learned, what action they took, and what questions they still have.

Resource 21 is a form that will help students stay focused and offer ideas for what they may want to share in their presentations, such as their LAQ, information about their product, how they shared their work with an authentic audience, and any roadblocks they had to work through over the course of their project.

Just as finding time to pitch ideas during class can be difficult, the same is true for presenting. Finding time for all students to present their projects can prove to be very difficult, especially as students finish their projects at different times. Remember, I shared Flipgrid as a solution to this problem when pitching, and the same tool can be used for presenting. Set up a grid for students to share their LAQ in a 2–3-minute presentation when they are ready. This will make presentation opportunities more flexible and give students a chance to share and move on rather than having to wait for everyone to finish so that they can all present on the same day.

RESOURCE 21
Presentation Planning Form

LAQ

L What Did I Learn?	A What Action Did I Take?	Q What Questions Do I Still Have?

What was your product?

_____

_____

_____

_____

_____

How did you share your work with the world?

_____

_____

_____

_____

_____

Resource 21: Presentation Planning Form, *continued*

Look back at your potential roadblocks. Were these a problem, and how did you over-come them?

_____

_____

_____

_____

_____

Major Successes	Epic Failures

Resource 21: Presentation Planning Form, *continued*

What did you learn about yourself?

_____

_____

_____

_____

_____

What are you most proud of?

_____

_____

_____

_____

_____

What would you do differently if you could do your project again?

_____

_____

_____

_____

Giving feedback on presentations is an important part of the process. Allowing students to hear from their peers, outside experts, school administrators, or others in the community is a crucial opportunity. Resource 22 is a form that can be used as you ask for that feedback.

Taking presentations to the next level involves sharing them beyond the walls of the classroom. Sharing what was learned with an authentic audience makes the process real and helps learners make connections. If your learners have found a way to create change or make an impact, big or small, they should share their story with the world. Doing so will give them reason to invest and will provide even more purpose as they prepare their presentations to share. As I've stated many times throughout the book, acquiring permission for them to share is necessary. Sharing work takes the project to a new level and helps students see the power of using social media or other outlets to positively promote work. You can also refer to Resource 23: Rules for Sharing Work Online as a student handout or classroom poster.

RESOURCE 22

Presentation Feedback Form

Project Title: _____

1. What did you learn from the presentation?

_____

_____

_____

_____

2. What do you still wonder?

_____

_____

_____

_____

3. What do you think the presenter did well?

_____

_____

_____

_____

4. What is one thing that the presenter could improve?

_____

_____

_____

_____

RESOURCE 23
Rules for Sharing Work Online

1. Share first names only.

2. Never mention where you live or where you go to school.

3. Always ask permission before sharing.

4. Be willing to accept feedback and suggestions.

5. Never engage in conversation without adult supervision.

6. Use social media to share positive information.

7. Think about the consequences before sharing anything online.

8. Know your audience, and remember that your work will be shared.

9. Talk to an adult if you see or receive anything inappropriate online.

10. Don't post pictures of friends or family members without permission.

Ready-to-Use Resources for Genius Hour in the Classroom © Taylor & Francis Group

Taking Genius Hour to the Next Level

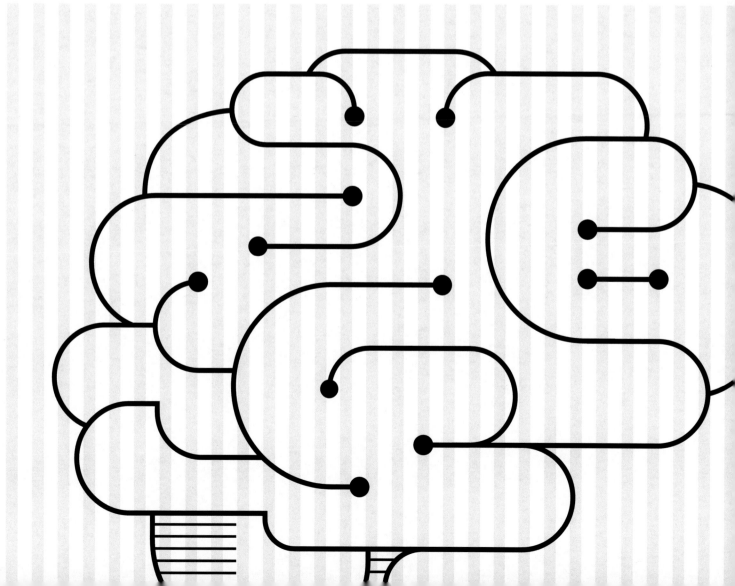

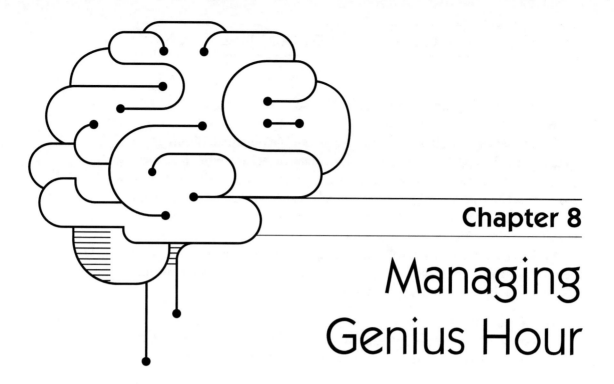

Chapter 8

Managing Genius Hour

Using Flipgrid to Manage the Process

I mentioned Flipgrid earlier in this book and want to help you understand how it can be used to design a meaningful process that works. Remember that if something you are doing in your classroom isn't manageable, it will more than likely not be meaningful. Using a tool like Flipgrid can give just enough structure that students will understand the process so that you can spend your time weaving in connections to content and life-ready skills.

Creating a Genius Hour grid involves a little bit of frontloading, but once it is created, it can be used over and over. One of the benefits of using Flipgrid is that you are able to duplicate a grid, meaning that once you create the grid, you can recreate it as many times as you need to for as many classes as you need to.

Not long ago, a fellow Genius Hour educator, Ethan Silva, shared with me on Voxer how he was hoping to use Flipgrid as he began to implement Genius Hour in his sixth-grade classroom. After listening and thinking about the role Flipgrid could play in Genius Hour, I thought about how perfect it would be to create a 6 P's of Genius Hour grid that could be used by students as a roadmap and opportunity to share their work throughout the process.

As I considered this option, I couldn't help but think about the huge role that reflection plays in Genius Hour and how powerful video reflection is for our learners. What a perfect fit! I instantly thought about the 6 P's of Genius

75

DOI: 10.4324/9781003237600-8

Hour and how educators could set up a Flipgrid to use throughout the entire process.

So, needless to say, after really thinking about the potential this might have to make the 6 P's of Genius Hour even more manageable and more meaningful, I jumped onto Flipgrid and created a Genius Hour grid, just to see what it might look like and how easy it might be to create. I created the grid in about 10 minutes and could not wait to share how to create a place for students to share and reflect throughout the Genius Hour process.

As you can see in Figure 2, I created one grid and a topic within that grid for each of the 6 P's. In the topic description, I asked questions that students might answer when they posted their video to the grid.

- **Passion:** What do you want to learn about? What do you think is interesting? What can you get excited about? *Students could also share their Thrively results here or even post a picture of their passion bracket.*

- **Plan:** Who will be your outside expert? What materials will you need to complete the project? What will you need to do each day to reach your goals? How much time will you need?

- **Pitch:** How will you share your idea with the class? How will you get us on board? What do you know? What do you want to know? How will you find out (KWH)?

- **Project:** What did you learn today? What connections did you make, and what would you like to share? *You might include the link to the Reflection QR code here so that students can respond to the question that they randomly receive. You could also attach the QR code as an image, and students could scan to receive their question.*

- **Product:** What did you create? What can you show us to demonstrate your learning? If you were unable to create a product, what could you have done differently?

- **Presentation:** How do you plan to share your learning? Can you share your idea or project with others? What tools will you use to make your presentation engaging for the audience? What did you learn? What action did you take? What questions do you still have (LAQ)?

As students move through the process, they can post their thoughts, reflections, and responses on the grid. This gives them the ability to pitch, present, and reflect anytime from anywhere. This takes away the need for the teacher to always keep up with who needs to pitch and who needs to present. Students

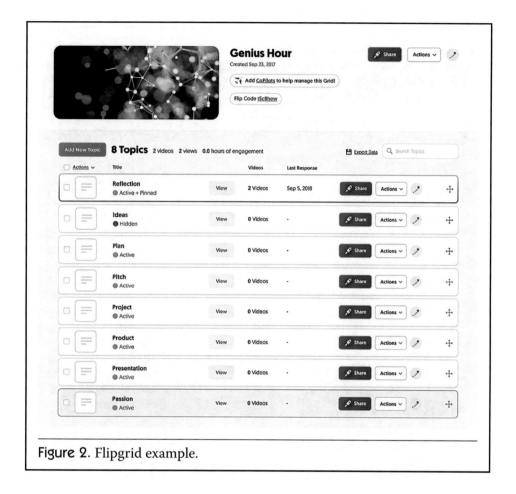

Figure 2. Flipgrid example.

can simply complete their tasks on Flipgrid whenever they are ready instead of waiting for a time in class that works for everyone.

Using Flipgrid also gives everyone an opportunity to respond and give feedback on Genius Hour projects. Flipgrid allows students to share pitches and presentations beyond the walls of the classroom, giving students an authentic audience. Grids can be shared with anyone whom you want to give access. You could give access to administrators, community members, outside experts, or the world. Anyone who has access will be able to give feedback, and that feedback will be beneficial for your learners.

In my classroom, the QR codes on the bulletin board in Figure 3 linked to the website that walked students through what to do for each of the 6 P's. I had to create a website, add all of the content, and then link the QR code to the different pages within the website. Using Flipgrid, you can simply put all of this information in the grid by clicking Actions, Share Topic, and choosing QR code. Copy the QR code, paste it onto cardstock, create the bulletin board, and it's done—so easy and very cool!

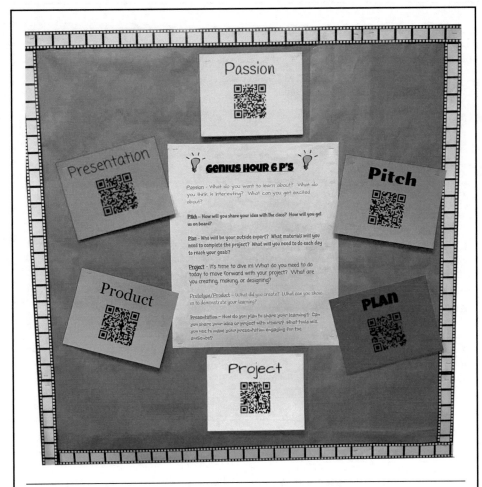

Figure 3. My classroom's Genius Hour bulletin board.

The Genius Hour QR Codes

As I have traveled and talked to many people about the Genius Hour bulletin board that I created for my classroom, I have been asked over and over if those QR codes were available to be used in any classroom. Unfortunately, I simply couldn't share them because the website had been created for my students. The forms and everything involved connected to my Google account, and it wouldn't work to give the address out to educators all over the country.

Just recently, I finally decided to create QR codes that can be used by any educator (see Resource 24: Genius Hour QR Codes). Each code links to a website that includes a video message from me to your learners as well as resources and ideas for them to use as they work through that specific part of the process.

Passion

What do you want to learn about?
What do you think is interesting?
What can you get excited about?

Plan

Who will be your outside expert?
What materials will you need
to complete the project?
How much time do you think
the project will take?

Pitch

How will you share your
idea with the class?
How will you get us on board?

Project

What do you need to do today
to move forward?
What are you creating, making,
or designing?

Product

What did you create?
What can you show us to
demonstrate your learning?

Presentation

Can you share your idea or
project with others?
What tools will you use to make your
presentation engaging for the audience?

This gives learners an opportunity to own their learning and find their own way through the process so that you, the teacher, can spend your time helping your learners connect to content and life-ready skills as they learn through application.

This system can be created by any teacher in any classroom. You certainly don't have to use my QR codes. I just wanted to create something that might jumpstart your Genius Hour journey so that you can get started as quickly and as easily as possible. Feel free to use the QR codes in whatever way is best for your learners. You can use them as an example as you create your own website, or simply use them as-is and allow your learners to access the videos and content that I've created as they move through the 6 P's of Genius Hour. Do what works for you and your learners. There is no right or wrong.

Using Book Creator or Google Slides to Make the Process Manageable

Having a place to document what students are learning and what they have done as they move through the process is important. I have known about Book Creator (https://bookcreator.com) for some time but just recently considered what it might look like to use this tool to organize the Genius Hour process.

I began by creating an account and setting up my library. Next, I chose my book size and created a page for each one of the 6 P's. As the educator, you can create a template for your students to use. They simply use the code to your library to access the book, make a copy, and then add their content. You can set the book up in a way that works for you and your learners. In Figure 4, I've shared an example of what that could look like.

In this same way, you could create a template on Google Slides and encourage students to make a copy before editing the master. You can force a copy of the slides by deleting the word *edit* on the end of the address and changing it to the word *copy*. I like the idea of using Google Slides because of the opportunity to collaborate and share so easily. You could add images and cool fonts to make the template fun or even encourage your learners to create their own templates and their own books if they are old enough to do so.

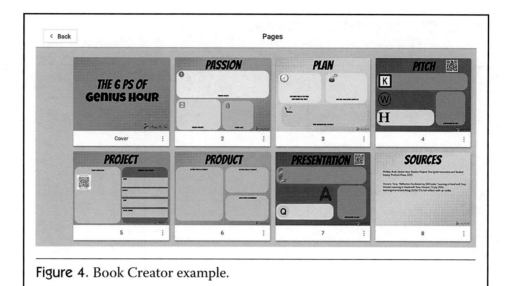

Figure 4. Book Creator example.

Assessing Genius Hour

I often get asked about grading Genius Hour. I've always said that I think it's important not to grade Genius Hour because, let's face it, how do you put an 85% on someone's passion? That being said, I also understand the importance of feedback and helping students understand what they've done well and what they need to work on.

I recently stumbled upon the idea of the single-point rubric from Jennifer Gonzalez, the author of the blog and host of the podcast Cult of Pedagogy. Although the post was from 2015, it was my first time to read about the idea, and the single-point rubric made so much sense as a possibility for giving students feedback on Genius Hour projects. Resource 25 is a rubric that can be used with the 6 P's to do just that.

I'm not a fan of traditional rubrics, as I just feel like they require so much time and force educators to fit elements of a project into a box. I've judged Genius Hour projects before, and when using a rigid rubric, I have difficulty giving authentic feedback. I find myself trying so hard to decide whether a student's work fits in the 1, 2, 3, or 4 box that I'm unable to find the time to tell the student what I think he or she did well and not so well. Enter the single-point rubric. I love this idea so much because it is simple and allows for authentic feedback that will be most beneficial for the learner. Rather than focusing on which box to check, I am able to identify what I believe would be proficient and then give feedback based on my concerns and evidence of exceeding expectations.

RESOURCE 25

Genius Hour Single-Point Rubric

Concerns (Areas of Concern)	The 6 P's	Advanced (Evidence of Exceeding Expectations)
	Passion: Passion is well-defined and grounded in purpose. Learner has a solid project idea and has identified the why behind the project. Project idea is focused on creating change or making an impact beyond the walls of the classroom.	
	Plan: Learner identified (1) how long the project will take, (2) what materials will be needed, and (3) who the outside expert will be. Plan has been carefully considered and seems realistic.	
	Pitch: Pitch was creative and communicated well. The learner shared his or her KWH (what is known, what he or she wants to know, and how he or she will find out). Technology was used well, and the pitch was clear and concise.	

Resource 25: Genius Hour Single-Point Rubric, *continued*

Concerns (Areas of Concern)	The 6 P's	Advanced (Evidence of Exceeding Expectations)
	Project: Learner values and demonstrates the power of reflection while working on the project. Time is used wisely, and the learner is making connections to content while working on the project. Standards are consistently documented, and the learner is willing to collaborate with others in order make connections and reach a deep level of understanding.	
	Product: The product represents what was learned throughout the Genius Hour process. The learner created something or learned something valuable throughout the process that can be showcased and shared.	
	Presentation: Presentation was creative and communicated well. The learner shared his or her LAQ (what was learned, what action was taken, and what questions remain). Technology was used well, and the presentation was clear and concise.	

Let's compare student projects to the different types of steak that many people enjoy. A medium project is fine. It's not over the top, but there's no reason for concern. It's fine, meaning the learner did what was expected, nothing more and nothing less. A well-done project is just that. Maybe extra time was spent, innovation was involved, or a fresh perspective was shown. In other words, the learner did more than was expected and demonstrated a deep understanding of the learning along the way.

Think about an undercooked steak. It doesn't take long to prepare, doesn't always look great (to those of us who prefer well done), and can leave a bad taste in your mouth. The same is true for a project that does not meet expectations. Although we want to be flexible and give our learners as much freedom as possible, it's okay to help them understand what needs to be in place in order for a project to be well done.

The most important piece of assessing Genius Hour or giving feedback is to involve the learner. I think it's a good idea for both the teacher and learner to complete the rubric. Then, they can come together to compare notes. Often times, students are harder on themselves than teachers are on them, especially when a number grade isn't involved. Take time to see the project from their perspective and give them the opportunity to see it from yours. In doing so, you will build relationships and help your learners understand how to step back and see their own work for what it is.

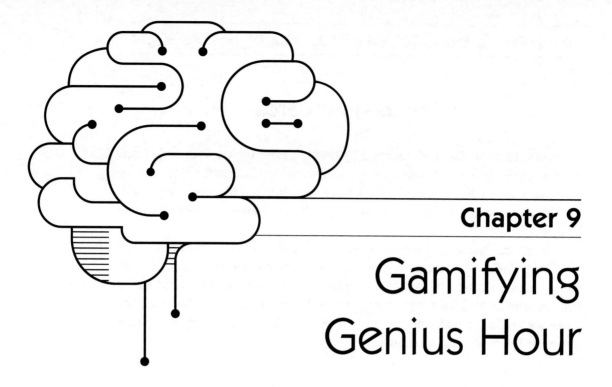

Chapter 9

Gamifying Genius Hour

Gamification is defined as the application of typical elements of game playing (e.g., point scoring, competition with others, rules of play) to other areas of activity. Using this definition, it's easy to think of some very practical ways that we can gamify Genius Hour for our learners. I think you have to be careful because Genius Hour shouldn't be competitive. However, you can definitely apply some of the typical elements of game playing into the process to make Genius Hour more fun and engaging for students as they move through each of the 6 P's.

Pick a card, any card. Being intentional about weaving in life-ready skills and content into passion-based learning is not always an easy task. It's easy to get so wrapped up in finding outside experts, identifying passions, and gathering materials that everything else is easily forgotten.

In an effort to help both educators and students be intentional about weaving in content and life-ready skills, I've created cards and a gameboard that can be used in the classroom to encourage them to do so. I wanted this part of Genius Hour to be simple but fun. I didn't want to gamify the process in a way that would cause learners to rush through the process or miss opportunities to make connections that need to be made.

DOI: 10.4324/9781003237600-9

Genius Hour Cards

Resource 26 includes content and life-ready cards. The cards include icons for the following content areas: art, science, social studies, math, English language arts and reading (ELAR). The cards also include the life-ready skills: collaboration, communication, creativity, critical thinking, reflection, and kindness.

During the Project portion of Genius Hour, students can simply draw a card from both stacks. They must find a way to weave the content and life-ready skill into what they are working on that day. This doesn't mean that they don't weave in other content and skills when the opportunity presents itself. It simply means that they are intentional and focused on weaving in the skills that are represented by the cards that are drawn.

Genius Hour Gameboard

The gameboard (see Resource 27) is very similar. However, instead of drawing a card, students roll a die and move the number of spaces that is rolled. The square that they land on represents the content area or life-ready skill that should be intentionally woven into their work that day. Again, this doesn't mean that they don't weave in other content and skills. It just challenges them to find a way to weave in a specific content area or life-ready skill.

You'll notice that the gameboard doesn't have a finish line and students have options on the different paths they might take. This board isn't meant to encourage competition or dictate what learners do during their Genius Hour Product time. Instead, it should help them think beyond just working on a project and help them make connections and intentionally apply their learning.

Genius Hour Dice

Finally, I've created a die for the life-ready skills and content areas (see Resource 28). The die can be rolled and used in the same way the cards and gameboards are used. This die is just another option and another way for you to encourage your learners to weave these skills and content areas into their learning experience as they work on their Genius Hour projects.

RESOURCE 26

Genius Hour Cards

COLL

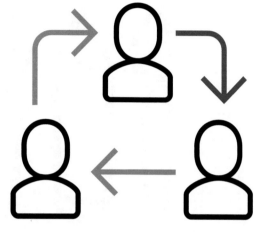

COMM

CR

CR TH

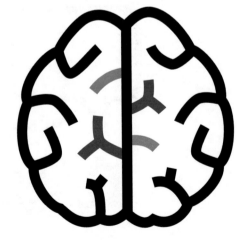

REF

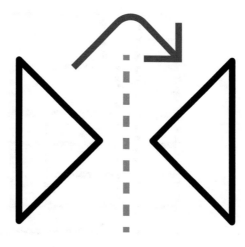

KIND

MATH

SCIENCE

ART

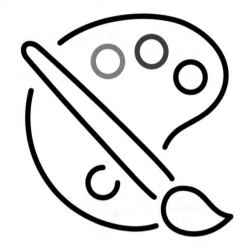

ELAR

TECHNOLOGY

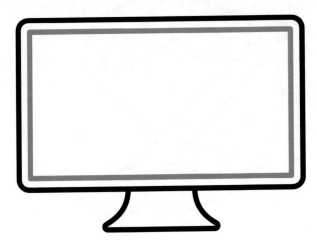

SOCIAL STUDIES

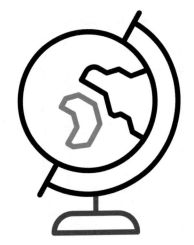

RESOURCE 27

Genius Hour Game Board

SOCIAL STUDIES	**TECHNOLOGY**	**CR**	**COMM**	**SCIENCE**
COLL				**REF**
REF	**ELAR**	**MATH**	**CR TH**	**ART**
KIND	**Genius Hour**			**COLL**
SCIENCE	**COMM**	**SOCIAL STUDIES**	**ART**	**KIND**
COLL				**CR TH**
CR	**MATH**	**ELAR**	**TECHNOLOGY**	**COMM**

RESOURCE 28

Genius Hour Die

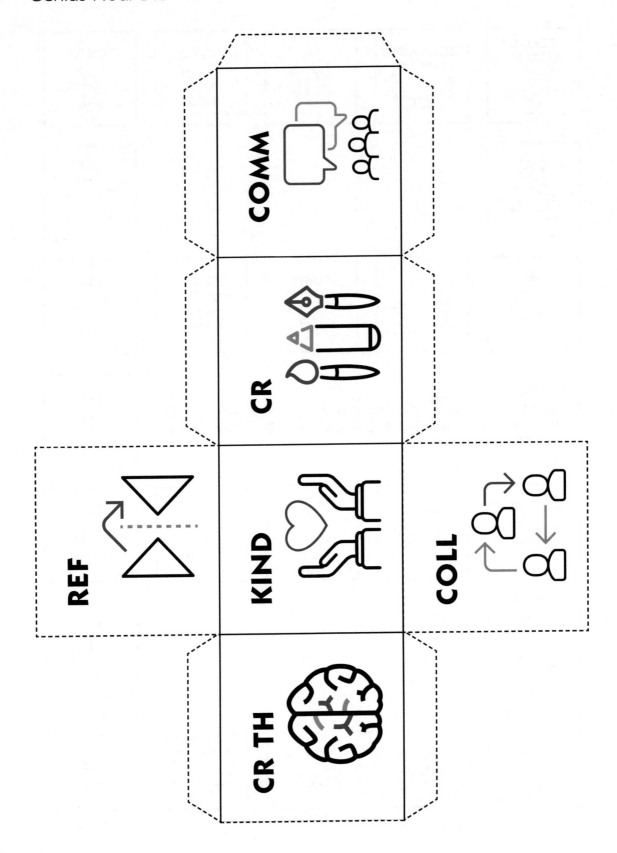

The 6 P's of Genius Hour Dice

You are going to have students who will say things like, "I don't know what to do," or "I don't know where to start." In an effort to help them find their way, I've created the 6 P's of Genius Hour Dice (see Resource 29). Although giving students the freedom and flexibility to own the learning and design their own projects is important, it's not a bad idea to have a Plan B for those who get stuck.

These dice are meant to be used as a backup plan. In other words, when a student isn't sure what to do or where to start, he or she can roll the dice for an idea. The dice can also be used for students who tend to want to do the same thing over and over again. Rolling the dice will force them to try new things and step outside of their comfort zones to learn about new tools and explore new ideas.

You'll notice that there are four original dice. One will look familiar, as it is the die that was suggested to use with reflection. Because reflection is the most important piece of the project part of Genius Hour, I think it's a good idea to just use the same die. The Pitch and Presentation dice are also the same, as these two parts of the process are very similar. Even if you've decided to use Flipgrid for students to pitch and present, they can attach what they create using these tools to their post on Flipgrid, and it will be accessible to those who see their post.

Consider printing several copies of the dice on different colored cardstock and keeping them in your classroom for your learners to access. Explain to students that the dice don't have to be used but are there in case they get stuck or need a springboard for an idea. I hope that you find these helpful and easy to implement in your classroom.

Utilizing the Gamification Resources

All of these options can be placed in different student groups for them to share. You can create as many as you need to be used in your classroom in a way that makes sense and is manageable for your learners. Remember, if something isn't manageable, it's difficult for it to be meaningful. Try using the different ideas and ask your students for feedback. Which do they prefer, or do they need any of them? Give them the opportunity to have some ownership in the Genius Hour experience and listen and react when they share their thoughts.

You probably won't have to use the cards or the gameboard for very long before students begin to really understand how to do this in a very authentic

RESOURCE 29

6 P's of Genius Hour Dice

Passion

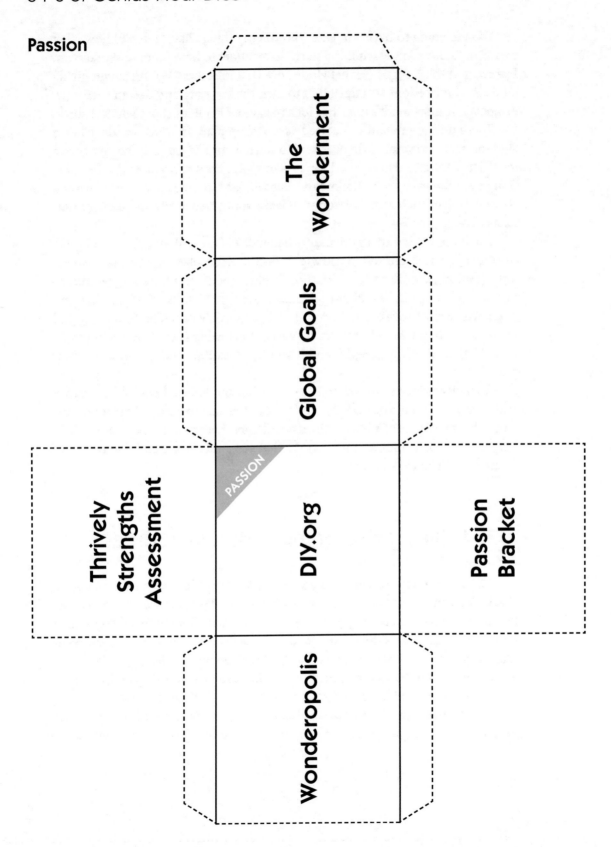

Resource 29: 6 P's of Genius Hour Dice, *continued*

Plan

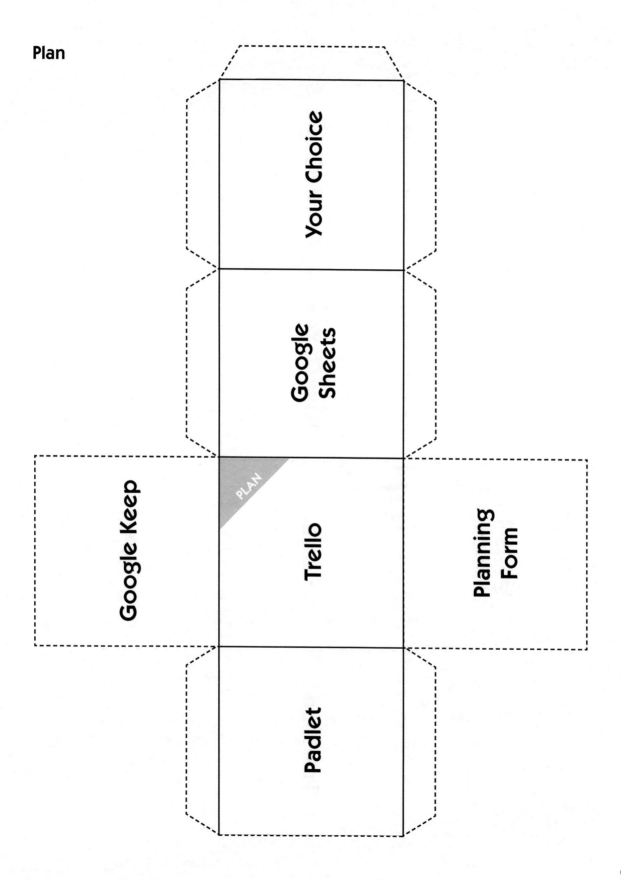

Resource 29: 6 P's of Genius Hour Dice, *continued*

Pitch

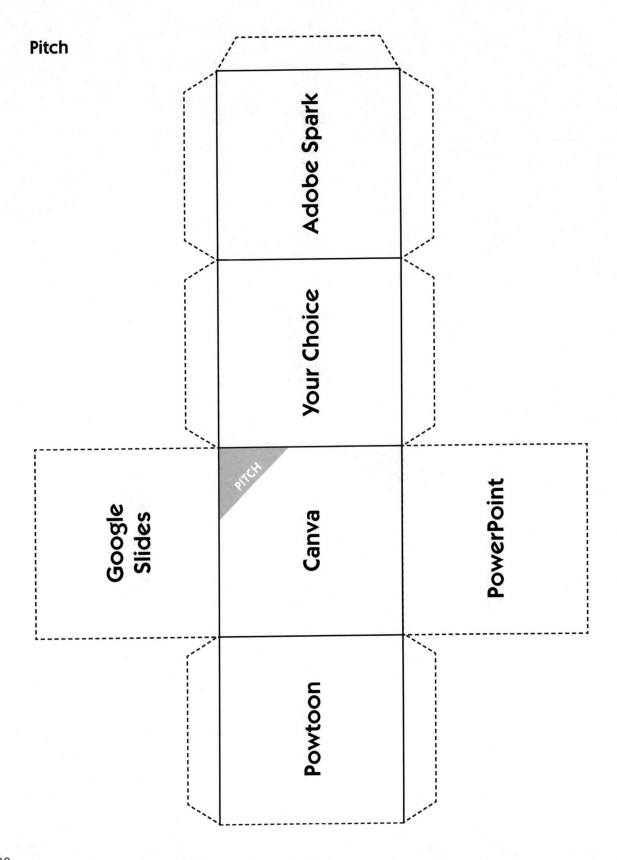

Resource 29: 6 P's of Genius Hour Dice, *continued*

Project

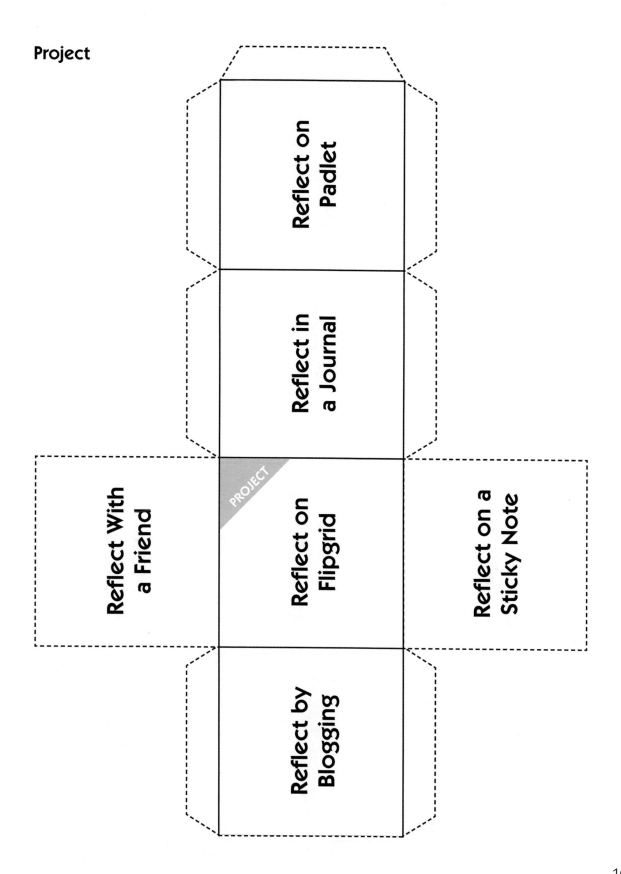

Resource 29: 6 P's of Genius Hour Dice, *continued*

Product

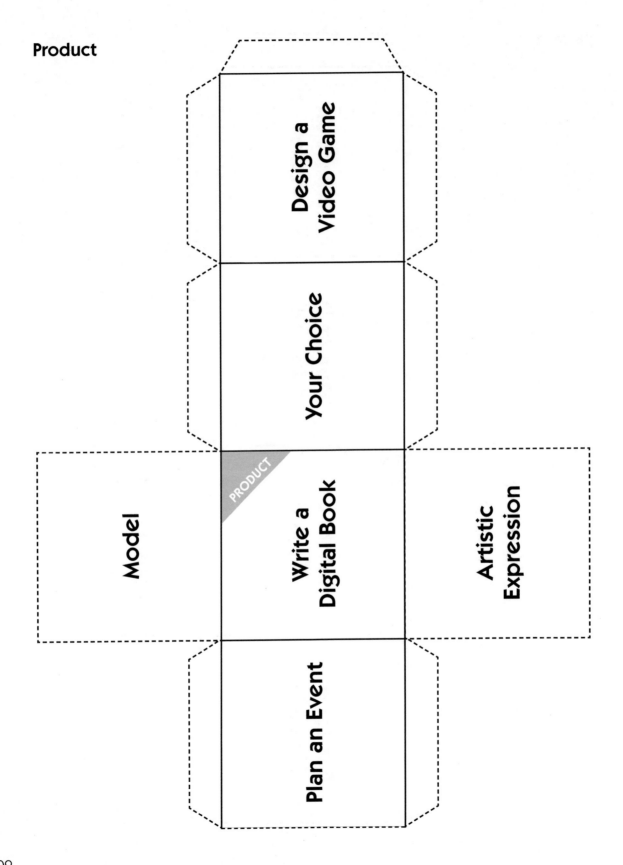

Resource 29: 6 P's of Genius Hour Dice, *continued*

Presentation

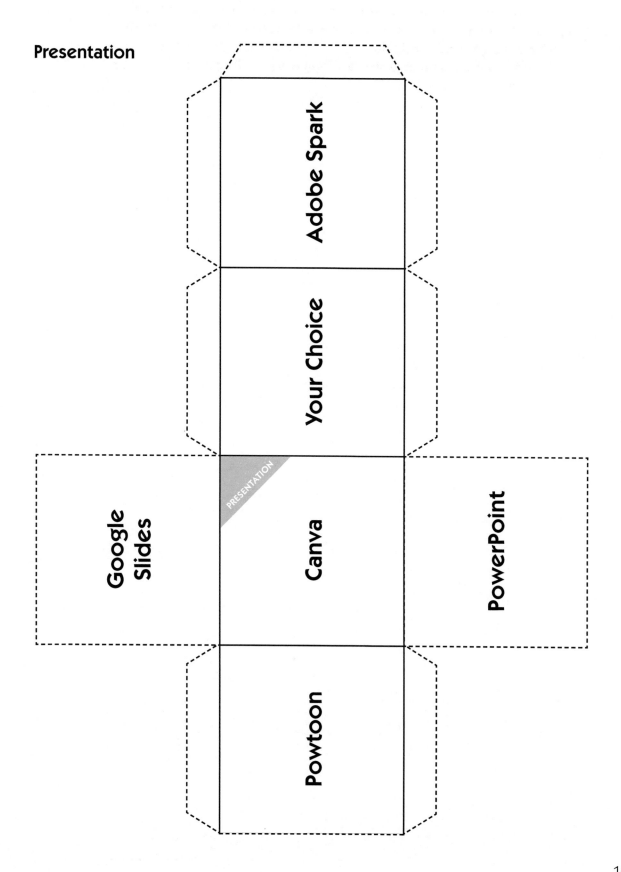

way. It will become second nature for them to realize when they are applying content and utilizing life-ready skills while working on their projects. These are simply training wheels to help them begin to think this way. Once they are able to do so without the cards or gameboard, they will be well on their way to learning through application.

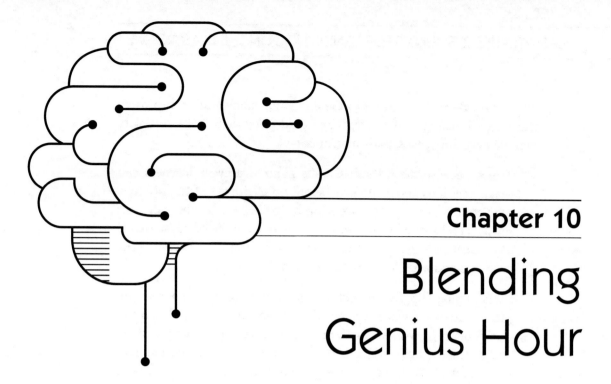

Chapter 10

Blending Genius Hour

Blended learning is quite the buzzword in education and something that is talked about as an effective way to engage and empower today's learners to take ownership of their learning. Blended learning is defined as:

> any formal education program in which a student learns at least in part through online learning, with some element of student control over time, place, path, and/or pace . . . at least in part in a supervised brick-and-mortar location away from home . . . [and] the modalities along each student's learning path within a course or subject are connected to provide an integrated learning experience. (Horn & Staker, 2017, pp. 34–35)

Let's take the definition apart and consider how you might be able to blend the Genius Hour experience for your learners:

1. **At least in part through online learning with some element of student control over time, place, path, and/or pace.** Obviously, most of Genius Hour involves online learning, as students are going to be researching personalized topics as they pursue their passions. Before doing the work on a project, they will need to find information and learn about their concept or idea in order to move forward. As discussed, students will also connect with experts beyond the walls of the

DOI: 10.4324/9781003237600-10

classroom. Because the 6 P's of Genius Hour allow students to drive their own learning experience, they could potentially have complete control over time, place, path, and/or pace.

- **Time:** Because the 6 P's of Genius Hour is a cycle, learners can make decisions about the time spent on each part of the process. One student may spend a week on his or her pitch, while another finishes and shares his or her thoughts in a couple of days. This is to be expected and gives learners the opportunity to become self-aware and do what works best for them.

- **Place:** Using Flipgrid gives students the opportunity to access the process from anywhere at any time. They don't have to be in the classroom to be working on their project and can make connections and post ideas using any device. This makes the learning real and helps students realize that, as my friend Don Wettrick (2014) said, opportunities are everywhere (p. 105).

- **Path:** Although the 6 P's of Genius Hour are a roadmap for the path to follow through the process, learners can have some control over what they explore within each of the P's. In other words, one student might use the Passion Bracket to find his or her passion while another explores DIY.org. This gives students control over their path while still following the roadmap so that they do not get lost.

- **Pace:** Students should be allowed to determine how long they think their projects will take. One learner may design a project that will take 3 weeks while another works on one that will take all year. Controlling their own pace gives them ownership and holds them accountable as they work toward meeting their goals and creating the change that they set out to impact.

2. **At least in part in a supervised brick-and-mortar location away from home.** I believe that much of Genius Hour should be completed in the classroom so that educators are able to observe and offer feedback to their learners. This means that Genius Hour shouldn't be assigned as homework. Students often already pursue their passions outside of the classroom. The goal of Genius Hour is to give students an opportunity to pursue their passions during the school day in an effort to help them learn by doing and make connections to the content as they learn through application.

3. **The modalities along each student's learning path within a course or subject are connected to provide an integrated learning experience.** Although this part of blended learning requires some intentionality on the part of the educator, it's another piece of blended learning that makes complete sense with Genius Hour. When we make a conscious effort to connect Genius Hour to our content, we help our students see innovation as a way to learn rather than a separate experience that is simply fun or engaging. Weaving the standards into a student's passion project helps him or her realize why it was important to learn a specific skill. It's no longer being learned because it's on the test but is seen as something that students can actually use beyond the walls of the classroom to reach their goals.

Tucker, Wycoff, and Green (2017) stated in their book, *Blended Learning in Action*, that when implemented successfully, blended learning enables several hallmarks of best teaching and learning practices, including personalization, agency, authentic audience, connectivity, and creativity. It's not a stretch to realize how each of these practices plays a role in the 6 P's of Genius Hour. Pursuing passions in order to experience real learning is a unique way for students to personalize their learning through making connections.

Strategies for Blending Genius Hour

One of the blended learning models shared in Tucker et al.'s (2017) book is the Station Rotation Model. In this model, students rotate through stations, one of which should involve online learning. This could be set up in your classroom using the 6 P's. In other words, you could have a station for each of the 6 P's in your classroom when it's time to implement Genius Hour. This way, students could collaborate with others who are working within that same part of the process and use similar tools and materials available at that station. This would also be an easy way for you as an educator to see how many students are working within each part of the process and be intentional as you walk around weaving in standards and life-ready skills.

Genius Hour could also be flipped using the Flipgrid suggestion mentioned previously in this book. Students could come to class completely prepared for what they will be working on by watching the explanation video created by the teacher on Flipgrid the night before. This experience would give learners complete control over the pace of their project. It would also give students an opportunity to watch the video more than once, if necessary, in order to really understand what is expected as they begin to work on that particular part of their Genius Hour project.

There are so many different ways that Genius Hour can be blended so that it works for you and your learners. Take time to consider what will work best and the impact it will have on your classroom. Chances are that you and your students will have to "test drive" several options before deciding on what works best. Keep the lines of communication open, listen to student feedback, and be willing to take risks. In doing so, you will eventually land upon a Genius Hour experience that works and works well for everyone involved.

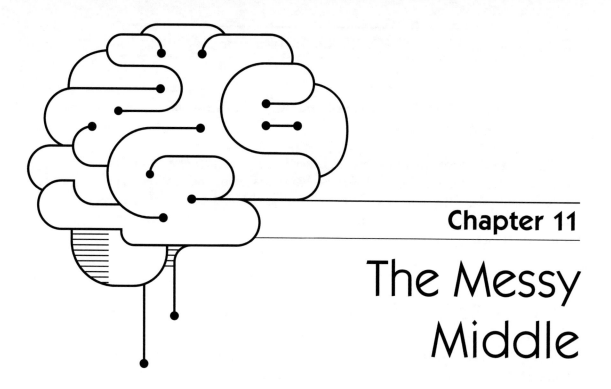

Chapter 11

The Messy Middle

I recently went back to visit with teachers who had implemented Genius Hour for several months. I had visited their campus and shared the 6 P's and was actually invited back to collaborate with grade-level groups so that they could ask questions and share their concerns. As I walked into the school for the day of collaboration, I knew what I was up against. I fully realized, based on when I had visited the first time and the amount of time that they had been given to implement Genius Hour, that they were in the "messy middle" of passion-based learning. They felt like they were doing it wrong, had tons of questions, and just felt like they had failed at what was supposed to be exciting and fun for their learners.

The messy middle is the part of Genius Hour that is uncomfortable for everyone. It feels as if you are doing it "wrong" because your students are not as excited as expected, they aren't creating amazing projects that can even compare to the projects that you've seen other teachers share on Twitter, and you are frustrated and tired. This, my friend, is the messy middle—and we've all been there.

Scott Belsky, author of *The Messy Middle*, said in a Medium article (2018) that:

> Every advance reveals a new shortcoming. Your job is to *endure* the lows and *optimize* the highs to achieve a *positive slope* within the jaggedness of the messy middle—so that, on average, every

DOI: 10.4324/9781003237600-11

low is less low than the one before it, and every subsequent high is a little higher. (para. 3)

This is exactly what has to happen in order to survive the messy middle and come out on the other side. Optimize the highs by sharing them, reflecting on them, and celebrating with your learners, colleagues, and administration. Endure the lows in the same way—share them, reflect on them, and celebrate the learning that happened because of the lows.

Reflect, Revise, Reach Out

It's hard to see the messy middle when you are in it. It's much easier to see when it's behind you. But just like quicksand, if you stay still, satisfied with the feelings you have right now and unwilling to continue moving forward, you will sink. And, if you sink, you will miss out on all of the wonderful that's on the other side. So, what does it look like to move forward? How can you continue to put one foot in front of the other when everything in you is telling you to throw in the towel? I have three pieces of advice . . .

1. reflect,

2. revise, and

3. reach out.

Reflect

Reflect on what happens every day during Genius Hour. Think about what is working and what's not. Write your reflections down. Start a blog, write in a journal, or talk with a friend. Use Resource 30 to get you started. Just reflect. Remember, John Dewey is often quoted as saying that, "We don't learn from an experience, we learn from reflecting on an experience." If this is true, then we will never learn how make things better if we don't take the time to reflect.

Also, take time to read your students' reflections. Ask them what they like and don't like about Genius Hour and what they think you might be able to do to make it better. Help them understand that although this type of learning will never be easy, you want it to be something that they look forward to and enjoy. When they share ideas, listen and be willing to implement their suggestions. They might not all work, but by at least giving them a try you show your learners

RESOURCE 30

Genius Hour Reflections

1. What went well today?

_____

_____

_____

_____

_____

2. What didn't go well today?

_____

_____

_____

_____

_____

3. What evidence did I see/hear/experience of real learning?

_____

_____

_____

_____

4. What will I do differently next time?

_____

_____

_____

_____

that you are willing to really listen to them and take risks to find a way to make this work.

Revise

After you've reflected on what's working and what's not working, consider what you will do differently. How can you revise your practice to make it a better experience? The definition of *revise* is to reexamine and make alterations. Taking time to reflect is your opportunity to reexamine, and revising is about making the alterations. Don't be afraid to pivot. Try something new, do something different—just don't stay stuck in what isn't working. Remember, the first step in disrupting a system that doesn't work is to *stop doing what doesn't work*. Don't continue to do what isn't working simply because it was a suggestion in this book. Instead, find what works and go with it. And, when it stops working, find something new.

Reach Out

Finally, reach out to others. Being connected to other teachers who are implementing Genius Hour gives you a sounding board of people who actually understand what you are experiencing. I can't tell you how many times I've sat down with teachers who are using the 6 P's and we just laugh and say, "I know, right?" over and over. We get it and we get each other. There is something about sharing ideas and experiences with others who have walked in your shoes. It's refreshing and often results in solutions that can only be found through real collaboration.

The messy middle is real. Very few people are able to avoid it, and it's important that you don't throw in the towel. Be willing . . . willing to reflect, willing to revise, and willing to reach out. Doing these three things will make the messy middle easier and may even help you come out on the other side a lot faster than if you choose to stand still and do nothing. Hold onto the fact that you are giving your learners an opportunity that they deserve. Remember that by pursuing their passions, many of your learners are finding who they are. Consider the impact that this will have on the rest of their educational careers and even beyond. Because, when you take time to see the big picture, the messy middle seems pretty small and worth every single bit of struggle that it will require to overcome.

Section IV

Conclusion

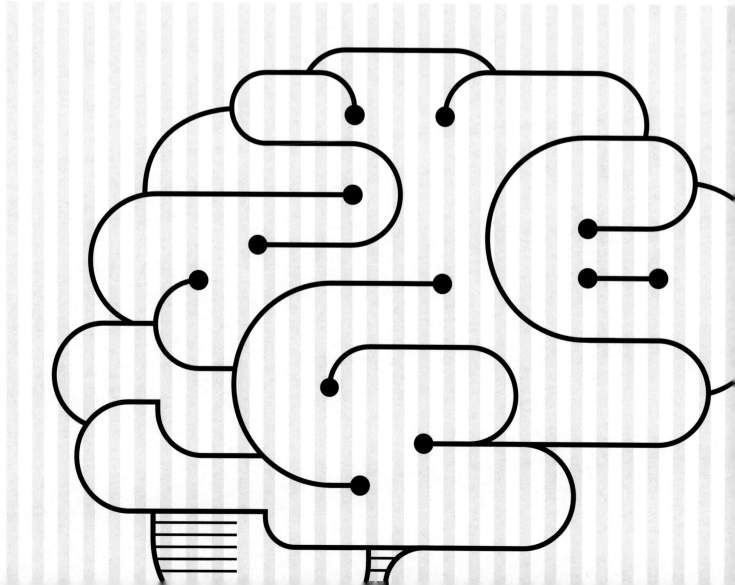

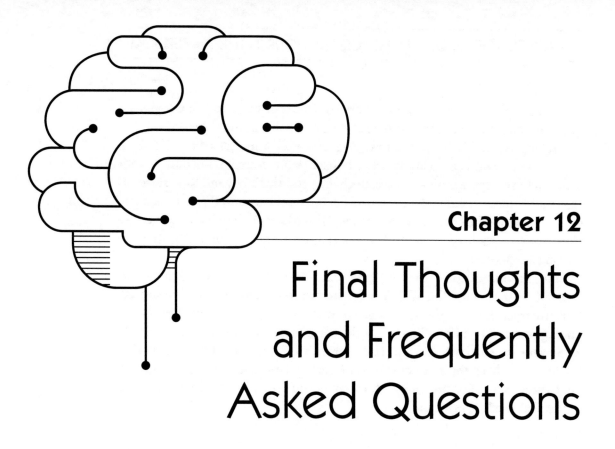

Chapter 12

Final Thoughts and Frequently Asked Questions

The 6 P's of Genius Hour were never meant to be a rigid plan for teachers to follow as they implement passion-based learning in their classrooms. Instead, the process is a roadmap for them to follow to make the process manageable for them and meaningful for their learners.

Think of it this way . . . if you were on a road trip with friends and planned on stopping in six major cities, chances are that you wouldn't all want to see the exact same things in every city. Even though you were in the same place, you would want to explore, see different things, make different stops, and learn different things from your experience. The same should be true for the 6 P's of Genius Hour. Although passion, plan, pitch, project, product, and presentation are the stops that you make along the way, they may not look the same in your classroom as they look in another.

Find what works for you and be flexible as you find what works for your learners. Prepare yourself to be frustrated, excited, confused, and inspired all at the same time. And expect the same from your learners. Genius Hour is outside of everyone's comfort zone and requires risk-taking and a willingness from both educators and students to learn together. Remember to push through the messy middle and share your experiences with others.

The #geniushour community on Twitter is such a great way to connect and share experiences with educators all over the world who believe in passion-based learning and have made it work in their own classrooms. This is also a

DOI: 10.4324/9781003237600-12

great place to find outside experts, share student projects, and just ask general questions about Genius Hour and what it can look like in the classroom.

Taking Genius Hour to the next level is simply a matter of moving from what product you can create to what impact you can make. Encourage your learners to see opportunities to create change and think beyond themselves as they find solutions and make an impact on the world around them. Help them understand that they don't have to change the world. By creating change in their classroom, on their campus, in their district, or in their community, they are making a difference.

By allowing purpose to drive projects, you will help your learners stay focused on their why. This will prevent the fire from fizzling and give you the tools that you need to the stoke the fire if it does begin to fizzle. Emphasize finding purpose and be willing to ask the hard questions. It will be difficult but wonderful, exhausting but inspiring, and frustrating—but worth it. Let's be willing to do the hard things to create real learning experiences for our students. So, I guess there's just one thing left to say as you prepare to take Genius Hour to the next level . . . game on!

Genius Hour FAQ: Frequently Asked Questions

Q: What do I do with students who do not want to participate in Genius Hour?

A: Not all of your students will be excited about Genius Hour. Many of them will be hesitant to participate in something that doesn't result in a grade and is so far beyond what the typical experience is at school. I once had a teacher share with me that she doesn't make her learners participate. Because Genius Hour is theirs and it's not about compliance or receiving a grade, she gives her students the option to be an assistant if they don't want to work on their own project. She explained that they often realize assistants typically do what the student working on the project doesn't want to do, and they often choose to begin their own project shortly after.

Q: Are students allowed to quit in the middle of a project?

A: I allowed students to stop working on a project if they had truly realized that they were no longer passionate about the work. However, if they wanted to quit to avoid failure or because things got hard, that was a different story. I often think about companies that do not want you to unsubscribe from their services. In order to keep you from doing so, they often make it tedious or difficult to unsubscribe. If students really want to pursue a different project, it's a good idea to make them go through the process of reflecting on why they are switching projects and maybe even fill out a form to share that reflection. If they truly want to change, they won't mind going through this process.

Q: Should Genius Hour be graded?

A: I don't know how you give someone's passion an 85. However, I do believe that feedback should be given throughout the process, and this can be done using the rubric that was shared in Chapter 8. Using this rubric, you are able to address what needs to be improved upon and acknowledge what was done well. Giving Genius Hour a number will prove to be very difficult if not impossible.

Q: How long should a project take?

A: I didn't dictate how long my students were able to work on their projects. Every learner is different, as is every project that students choose to pursue. Try to hold your students accountable to their prediction in the planning part of Genius Hour. Although they shouldn't be expected to finish exactly on time, they should try to stay on course or at least be expected to explain when they aren't able to finish on time. My students had projects that lasted 3 weeks, and they also had projects that lasted all year long. It's simply a matter of how flexible you want to be in the process.

Q: Can Genius Hour be incorporated into content areas?

A: Of course! There are no rules when it comes to Genius Hour. Do what you need to do to make it relevant in your classroom, and give your students opportunities to make connections to the content that you teach.

Q: Does Genius Hour have to be an hour?

A: Absolutely not! Make Genius Hour work for you and your learners. I know educators who do Genius Hour twice a week, once a week, once a every 6 weeks, or twice a year. Any time that students are given to pursue their passions is better than no time at all. Obviously, my hope is that they are able to do this more often than not. I like the idea of focusing on Genius Hour once or twice a week, but it doesn't have to be an hour. Do what works for you and be willing to be flexible as you find ways to figure it all out.

Q: What if students are working on Genius Hour in another classroom? Should they have multiple projects?

A: I think this can get tricky, and I think the best idea is to collaborate as educators to give learners an opportunity to work on one project in both classes. Weave your content area into their learning when they are in your classroom, but tackling two passion projects would prove to be very difficult even for the most ambitious learners.

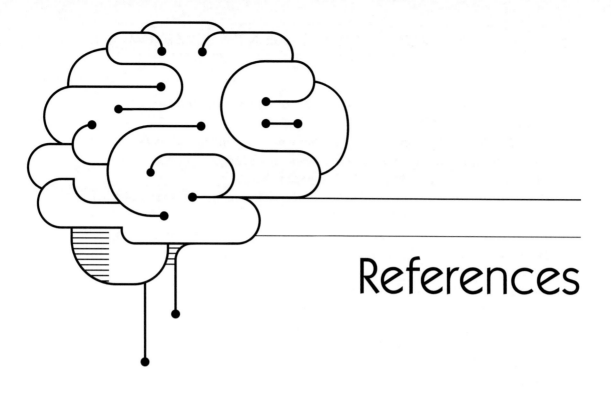

References

Belsky, S. (2018). Navigating the messy middle. *Medium*. Retrieved from https://medium.com/positiveslope/navigating-the-messy-middle-7ca6fff11966

Bloom, B. (Ed.). (1956). *Taxonomy of educational objectives: The classification of educational goals. Handbook I: Cognitive domain.* New York, NY: Longmans Green.

Buchanan, A. (2016). A new psychology for a new economy: The benefit mindset. *Medium*. Retrieved from https://medium.com/benefit-mindset/a-new-psychology-for-a-new-economy-the-benefit-mindset-241d0cc4c887

Derby, J. L. (2014). The difference between passion and purpose (and why you need both). *Pick the Brain*. Retrieved from https://www.pickthebrain.com/blog/difference-passion-purpose-need/

Dweck, C. (2006). *Mindset: The new psychology of success.* New York, NY: Ballantine Books.

Gonzalez, J. (2015). *Meet the #singlepointrubric* [Web log post]. Retrieved from https://www.cultofpedagogy.com/single-point-rubric

Horn, M. B., & Staker, H. (2017). *Blended: Using disruptive innovation to improve schools.* San Francisco, CA: Jossey-Bass.

Juliani, A. J. (2013). *6 simple strategies to help find your passion* [Web log post]. Retrieved from http://ajjuliani.com/6-simple-strategies-to-help-find-your-passion

Kirr. J. (n.d.). *Genius hour/20% time.* Retrieved from https://www.livebinders.com/play/play?id=829279#anchor

McNair, A. (2017). *Genius hour: Passion projects that ignite innovation and student inquiry.* Waco, TX: Prufrock Press.

McNair, A. (2019). *A meaningful mess: A teacher's guide to student-driven classrooms, authentic learning, student empowerment, and keeping it all together without losing your mind.* Waco, TX: Prufrock Press.

McTighe, J., & Wiggins, G. (2013). *Essential questions: Opening doors to student understanding.* Alexandria, VA: ASCD.

Mind Tools Content Team. (n.d.). SMART goals: How to make your goals achievable. *Mind Tools.* Retrieved from https://www.mindtools.com/pages/article/smart-goals.htm

National Education Association. (2010). *Preparing 21st century students for a global society: An educator's guide to the "four Cs".* Retrieved from http://www.nea.org/assets/docs/A-Guide-to- Four-Cs.pdf

Project Everyone. (n.d.). *The global goals for sustainable development.* Retrieved from https://www.globalgoals.org

Schneider, F. (2018). Fast goals—why FAST is better than SMART for your goals. *Workpath.* Retrieved from https://www.workpath.com/en/magazine/fast-goals-why-fast-is-better-than-smart-for-your-goals

Stanny, B. (2012). A fascinating new concept: How "thought partners" add value to your business. *Forbes.* Retrieved from https://www.forbes.com/sites/barbarastanny/2012/06/19/a-fascinating-new-concept-how-thought-partners-add-value-to-your-business/#7d9d8b981353

Tucker, C. R., Wycoff, T., & Green, J. T. (2017). *Blending learning in action: A practical guide toward sustainable change.* Thousand Oaks, CA: Corwin.

Vincent, T. (2013). Reflection facilitated by QR codes. *Learning in Hand.* Retrieved from http://learninginhand.com/blog/2013/7/5/roll-reflect-with-qr-codes

Watanabe-Crockett, L. (2018). *2 simple things that will make essential questions better every time* [Web log post]. Retrieved from https://www.wabisabilearning.com/blog/2-things-make-essential-questions-better

Wettrick, D. (2014). *Pure genius: Building a culture of innovation and taking 20% time to the next level.* San Diego, CA: Burgess Consulting.

YourDictionary. (n.d.). *Examples of measurable goals and objectives.* Retrieved from https://examples.yourdictionary.com/examples-of-measurable-goals-and-objectives.html

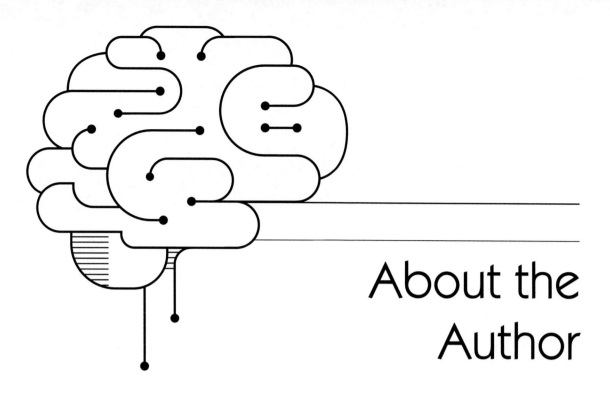

About the Author

Andi McNair is the Digital Innovation Specialist at ESC Region 12 in Waco, TX. Before working at the center, she taught elementary and gifted/talented students at a small rural school in Texas. Andi was in the classroom for a total of 16 years before pursuing her passion to change education by giving educators practical ways to create experiences that will engage and empower this generation of learners. Andi has spoken at many conferences and education service centers, and has worked with many school districts to provide innovative learning experiences for their students. She was named one of the Top People in Education to Watch in 2016 by the Academy of Education Arts and Sciences. Andi's first book, *Genius Hour: Passion Projects That Ignite Innovation and Student Inquiry*, is winner of the 2019 Teachers' Choice Award for Professional Development.